soulsister

respect

Jessie Minassian

Regal

Ventura, California, U.S.A.

Gospel Light is a Christian publisher dedicated to serving the local church. We believe God's vision for Gospel Light is to provide church leaders with biblical, user-friendly materials that will help them evangelize, disciple and minister to children, youth and families.

It is our prayer that this Gospel Light resource will help you discover biblical truth for your own life and help you minister to youth. May God richly bless you.

For a free catalog of resources from Gospel Light, please contact your Christian supplier or contact us at 1-800-4-GOSPEL *or* www.gospellight.com.

PUBLISHING STAFF
William T. Greig, Publisher • **Dr. Elmer L. Towns,** Senior Consulting Publisher • **Bayard Taylor, M.Div.,** Senior Editor, Biblical and Theological Issues

ISBN 0-8307-3799-5

Library of Congress Cataloging-in-Publication Data
Minassian, Jessie.
    Soul sister : respect / Jessie Minassian.
        p. cm.
    Includes bibliographical references and index.
    ISBN 0-8307-3799-5 (trade paper : alk. paper)
    1. Teenage girls—Religious life. 2. Teenage girls—Conduct of life. I. Title.
    BV4551.3.M56 2005
    248.8'33—dc22
                                                                            2005020779

table of contents

PART ONE:
Respect Your Body—
learning to dress
with dignity

one: the power of dignity

Strength and dignity are her clothing, and she smiles at the future.
Proverbs 31:25, *NASB*

Did you know that you are gorgeous—that you are one bea-u-ti-ful work of art?

Now, if you're like most teenaged girls, at this point you're probably thinking one of two things: (1) *This chick is nuts,* or (2) *Uh-oh, here it comes. Next she's going to tell me that God loves me "just the way I am." But if I'm so gorgeous, why won't* [insert the name of your latest crush] *even talk to me?*

If those thoughts sound familiar, you're not alone—most girls feel the same way at one time or another. We constantly compare ourselves to the girls we see on the covers of magazines and in movies—even to our circle of friends. These constant comparisons can make us feel miserable and self-conscious. Unfortunately, comparing ourselves to others can also keep us from just being ourselves, because we're always worrying about what other people think.

💬 **How do you feel about the way you look? Do you feel confident about the way you look, or do you ever wish that you could trade in your body for a swankier model?**

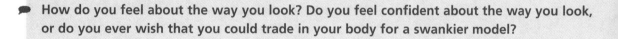

What Characteristics Do girls have?

Okay, now it's time for a pop quiz. I know, I know—we haven't known each other long enough for me to suggest such cruel punishment. But it won't be too painful, I promise. Just circle the word(s) you think fit best.

God designed female bodies to be

    a) Beautiful
    b) Unique
    c) Strong
    d) Nurturing
    e) Mysterious

I told you it would be painless. In fact, all the choices are correct. When God designed the first woman, Eve, He created her to be all these things in body, mind and spirit. And guess what? She complemented Adam, her male counterpart, very well. Adam must have been floored when he first met Eve! God wanted Adam—and every man after him—to have an intelligent, strong and sensitive friend in whom he could find joy and companionship.

What other fantastic characteristics do girls possess?

God knows all about these characteristics and more. Do you want to know what else God thinks about you?

- He made you in His image (see Genesis 1:27), and that's a great mold!
- He said that His creations, including females, were *very* good (see Genesis 1:31).
- God is concerned with the beauty of your heart (see 1 Samuel 16:7).
- He *personally* designed you from top to bottom. He knows every little detail about your design (see Psalm 139:13-16).
- He delights in you so much that He sings over you (see Zephaniah 3:17).
- He wants you to honor Him with the body He has given you (see 1 Corinthians 6:20).

are GIRLS AND GUYS different?

Guys and girls are different.

This concept shouldn't be a big surprise, but have you ever stopped to consider the differences between us and the other gender? Both the bodies and the emotional inner workings of guys and girls are *very* different, and I'm not just talking about the differences that you probably learned about in your junior high sex education course. The following chart highlights some of the physical differences between guys and girls. Try to think of more examples and add them to the bottom of the chart.

Guys	Girls
Angular features	Curved features
Rough skin	Smooth skin
More body hair; coarse	Less body hair; fine
Upper body strength	Lower body strength
Generally taller; weigh more	Generally smaller; weigh less
Described as "handsome"	Described as "beautiful"

💬 **What would the world be like if guys and girls were exactly the same?**

💬 **In what ways do you think God made the female body beautiful? You may have to think about this for a minute, but try to think creatively.**

💬 **Pull out your Bible and look up Song of Songs 7:1-9. Song of Songs is a love letter between a husband (who also happened to be Solomon, the king of Israel) and his beloved. What aspects of his beloved did Solomon find absolutely beautiful?** *(It's okay to giggle through your answers!)*

Wow, that's some serious love, right? Although Solomon's word choices seem a little weird ("your nose is like the tower of Lebanon"? Yikes!), we can tell that he was genuinely spellbound by every part of his beloved.

so, what's DIGNITY got to do with it?

Every girl possesses a mysterious charm *simply by being female*. If you're a girl (and if you're reading this book, I hope you are), your innate charm must be used the way God intended. This is where dignity comes in.

dignity (dig-ne-té) n—the quality or state of being worthy, honored or esteemed[1]

Dignity requires that you respect yourself enough to handle your body in a way that *God*, not man, will deem worthy. That's a high standard! Dignity applies to how you dress, how you act and even how you treat other people. The concept of dignity is also about respecting your future husband by deciding that you're a one-man woman. In this way, you make yourself worthy of honor, esteem and admiration. That's what having dignity is all about.

💬 **Are you convinced that you are one bea-u-ti-ful young woman? If not, explain why.**

💬 **Have you ever seen a girl act in a way that wasn't respectful of God or her future husband? Have *you* ever acted that way? Write about it.**

💬 **What do you think it means to reserve yourself for your future husband? Why do you think that is a good idea?**

HOW DOES SATAN LIE TO US?

Deep down, every girl wants to be admired, respected and honored, and that's what God wants for us too. He knows that when a girl holds her head high and walks with dignity, she is much happier and more confident as a person. Having dignity means that we can't treat others badly or throw ourselves at every cute guy who walks by. That's why Satan—our worst enemy—will do everything in his power to convince us that we'll get more respect from the world (and have more fun) if we forget about living with dignity and live every moment selfishly for ourselves.

One of Satan's favorite tools to confuse and frustrate us is the media. He uses magazines, movies, TV, billboards, catalogs, radio and anything else he can get his hands on to convince us that we have to act or look a certain way, that we can get whatever we want if we dress to get attention. Now, take a few minutes to answer the following questions.

- What lies do you think Satan tells us through the media to convince us that we aren't really worthy of dignity?

- Do you overlook the beautiful features of your body and instead focus on all the little things you wish you could change? What do you think is truly important, in God's eyes, when it comes to self-respect and dignity?

- Now, think about your favorite TV shows or movies. Describe the main female characters. Do they have dignity, or do they flaunt themselves for attention?

Okay, let's review: All girls possess a mysterious charm because that's the way God made them. We can either embrace that and walk with dignity (remember, dignity means living in a way that is worthy of honor, respect and admiration) or we can buy into Satan's lies, abuse our bodies, treat others disrespectfully and throw ourselves at every guy we see. The choice is ours to make. Will you pray with me?

> Awesome Creator, thank You for designing us to be strong, beautiful and totally unique women. Forgive me for not recognizing my own worth and for buying into Satan's lies that I'm not worthy of respect. Teach me to walk with the dignity You desire for me. I want to make You proud. Amen.

Note:

1. *Merriam-Webster's Collegiate Dictionary*, 11th ed., s.v. "dignity."

two: I can see clearly now

Fix your thoughts on what is true and honorable and right. Think about things that are pure and lovely and admirable. Think about things that are excellent and worthy of praise.
Philippians 4:8, *NLT*

A few years ago, I was a counselor for a group of junior high girls at a Christian outdoor education camp. We had a blast and no one went home with a cast!

In addition to great camp activities, such as cricket catching, arrow shooting, mud slinging and wigwam making, each morning the girls had to decorate the cabin according to the day's theme. And each morning, these girls went all out, let me tell you—balloons, streamers, posters, broom people—the place always looked terrific. Our cabin was a work of art, so I always tried to sneak back to the cabin before our first class to see what they had created while I was gone.

One morning the girls chose as their theme Proverbs 15:24: "The path of life leads upward for the wise to keep him from going down to the grave." As usual, they went over and above the call of duty. When I walked into the cabin, I saw that they had created two paths. The path that led to "life" was lined with happy, beautiful items that led to a treasure chest filled with their Bibles, crosses and WWJD (What would Jesus do?) bracelets. The other path led to "the grave" in the tiny bathroom, where they had arranged around the rim of the toilet every teen magazine they had brought with them (I'm still not sure how they got them all to stay on the toilets; these girls were good!).

I was proud of their handiwork, but then I got to thinking, *Wait a minute . . . they have been reading these magazines all week.* So that night, when they pulled out *Seventeen, Marie Claire* and *Cosmo Girl*, I asked, "If you think these magazines are worthy of lining the toilet, why do you read them?" None of them knew why.

💬 **Do you read any teen magazines? If so, which ones are your favorites? Why do you like to read them?**

I'm a big fan of fashion and makeup, and I know that those are two of the main reasons why girls say they read magazines such as *Seventeen*. So let's do an experiment. Grab the latest edition of your favorite magazine. Now, count how many pages are dedicated to giving you practical fashion and makeup tips. How many pages did you count?

How many pages are in the magazine?

Now, by doing some simple math (don't *even* reach for a calculator—you can do this), how many pages of the magazine *don't* contain fashion or makeup tips? (Count all the ads and all the articles.)

Just so you wouldn't think I was putting you through a cruel math-tutoring program, I did this experiment too. I just flipped through the latest copy of *Seventeen*, and here's what I found:

> Out of 181 pages,
> 36 had something to do with fashion (this was the "shopping issue," so most of these pages consisted of a few items of clothing with price tags and where to buy them),
> 18 were about beauty or makeup,
> 3 had to do with health, and
> 23 contained articles.

That left a whopping *101* pages for ads and an article about a bisexual boyfriend. So you tell me, if more than half of the pages of any given magazine aren't about what we buy them for, what are these magazines *really* selling to us?

💬 **Are you surprised how many pages of your magazine contain ads?**

💬 **Take a few minutes to look at some of the ads in your magazine. What sort of messages are those ads sending to you? Do you agree with those messages?**

AD CAMPAIGN

Did you know that the average person sees between 400 and 600 ads a day?[1] That means companies who want your business have some serious competition! If they're going to get you to buy their product instead of someone else's, their ads have to stand out from the rest. They know that the longer you look at their ad, the more likely you are to buy their product.

To find out what makes you look at ads for a longer time, advertising research firms have invented a device that can track where a person's eyes look on a page and how long the person looks at that section of the page. Advertising researchers spend a lot of time watching people's eyes move and trying to find ways to keep people looking longer. Bright colors and certain shapes and lines can make a person look at an advertisement up to 3 percent longer. But do you know what tops the charts? Advertising companies have found that if they place a picture of a beautiful woman in their ad, both men *and* women will look at that ad 14 to 30 percent longer![2] Crazy, huh?

- **Why do you think a picture of a woman is an advertiser's best friend? Why do you think a picture of a pretty lady makes us *girls* look longer at an ad?**

Big, obnoxious LIES

In the first session, we learned that God created females with a mysterious, indefinable quality that is charming to the opposite sex. Each girl is born with that inexplicable element of charm that makes her a girl.

Of course, Satan knows all about the appeal of a woman (remember, he was around when God made the first model), and he uses the media to twist that innocent beauty so that he can send us the lies he wants us to hear. I'm not pointing fingers at the ad agencies; they're just pawns in the devil's game. (Not that they're doing much to resist the temptation, but we'll leave them out of this for now.)

We're going to spend the rest of this session talking about four lies that Satan sends to us through the media—girls have been in the dark about his dirty tricks for too long. It's time we uncover him for the fraud he is so that we can live with dignity and hold our heads high.

Lie 1—You Must Look Like THIS to Be Beautiful

This lie is probably the most obvious of the four. Many TV shows, movies and magazines are filled with a certain "type" of girl. Oh, she may have different hair color or skin tone, but the main message comes out loud and clear.

- **If you were casting a movie and the main character was a perfect high school girl, what would she look like? Draw a picture of her in the box or, if you don't like to draw, just write your thoughts. Whether you draw or write, include details such as her height, weight, clothes, hair, makeup and facial features.**

I asked a few of my teenaged friends to share with me what they thought the "perfect" girl would look like. Here are some of their answers:

- Long, brown hair, around 5' 10" and size 8 clothes. She would have a creamy complexion and naturally long lashes.
- Curly or straight hair, 5' 7", thin, nice eyes and eyelashes, and a nice smile.
- Blonde, medium height, always latest style in clothes, tanned skin and thin (a size 6 or 8).

- Very thin, maybe a size C cup, and tall (at least 5' 8"). Her hair would be shiny and healthy, her makeup would always be perfect, and her skin would be tan year round.

Sound familiar? I'm willing to bet that at least some of their answers were similar to yours. Isn't it funny how practically every girl has the same idea of what a perfect girl would look like?

How do you think a girl who respects herself should respond to the pictures of "perfection" she sees all around her?

How can having dignity help you see past the lie that you have to look a certain way to be beautiful?

Lie 2—Our Product Will Give You Power

Now, here's a lie that's not as obvious but dangerous nonetheless. Satan knows that it's part of our human nature to want to be powerful. It has everything to do with a five-letter word spelled P-R-I-D-E. Satan knows that many of us girls especially like to have power over guys, and he plays on that desire like a four-string banjo. Let me give you an example.

A recent fashion ad shows a good-looking lad sleeping on his back in the middle of a jungle (on top of a banana leaf, of course, so that he doesn't spoil his brand-name khakis). A woman (who looks as though she hasn't eaten in months) stands over this unsuspecting guy with one foot strategically placed so that the heel of her gold stiletto shoe is right over the most vulnerable part of the man's body. She's got both hands on her bikini-clad hips, and it appears as if she's either about to eat the camera or is in some serious pain (hard to tell). She looks like a female rendition of Columbus, conquering the New World. Here's the message I'm hearing: Wear this designer's clothes and you'll be able to conquer any guy you want. Now, *that's* power. But is it true?

Here are a few more power-hungry phrases that I came across while I was browsing through a few magazines:

- Whatever your dark desires (printed under a picture of two obviously naked people)
- Strong and beautiful
- Find the strength you never knew you had
- How I Got the Guy (an article title)
- Leave him hot and bothered
- Empower your vision
- Rule #3—With a little practice you'll learn how to handle them (referring to guys)
- Don't mess with Miss S

Now, don't get me wrong, being emotionally and physically strong is not bad. The problem is that most of these ads depict these "strong" women wearing next to nothing. In essence, the ads are telling us, "If you're strong and powerful, you'll dress in less and show all the cleavage you can muster." We also run into trouble when we buy into the lie that being strong means dominating men.

🗩 **What's the danger in thinking that guys are just another thing to be had or conquered?**

🗩 **Do you think that you have to have power over guys or dress sexually to have dignity? (Remember, having dignity means earning the respect and admiration of others.) Why or why not?**

LIE 3—THE SEXIER YOU DRESS, THE MORE GUYS WILL LIKE YOU

This is a tricky one because this lie is *almost* true. Watch—I'll change only two small words and it will magically transform into a true statement. Ready? Abracadabra! The sexier you dress, the more guys will *lust after* you. That does change things, doesn't it? But most ad companies don't think puddles of boy drool will boost sales, so they opt not to include that part.

Because there are more examples of this type of lie in any one magazine than I could discuss in this entire book, I want you to pick up that magazine you had earlier and pick out three ads that show girls who look as though they're trying to seduce someone (it may be difficult to pick just three, but hang with me). If you're not sure what "seduce" means, just find the girls who look like they're about ready to eat you; you know, the ones you wouldn't trust within 50 feet of your boyfriend.

Now that you have picked three, let's answer a few questions about them.

- **What products are these ads selling? Do the products have anything to do with the ads? What are the advertisers *really* selling?**

- **Do the girls in these ads look friendly? Would you want to hang out with them? Would you let them anywhere *near* your boyfriend, your brother or a guy friend? Why or why not?**

- **If these pictures were part of a comic strip you were drawing, what words would you put in the speech bubbles? (e.g., "You want some of this?" or "This dress is giving me a serious wedgie—but man, I look hot!") Write on the actual ads you chose whatever words you think these ladies would say.**

- **If you were a guy looking at these ads, what would you think about these girls? Would you respect them or admire them? If you had one word to describe them, what word would you choose? (I'm guessing "dignity" wouldn't be your word of choice.)**

The bottom line is that dressing sexually doesn't give us dignity. In real life, if you dressed like the girls in the ads you chose, you'd have a lot of guys looking at you, but they would be looking for all the wrong reasons. We'll talk more in the next chapter about how the way we dress affects guys. But now, it's time for the next big, fat, obnoxious lie.

Lie 4—Physical Relationships Bring True Happiness

This lie is another one that is easy to miss at first glance. But once you know what to look for, such ads will become obvious to you. Go ahead—flip through your magazine and mark the pages that imply that you have to have a boyfriend (or at least a lot of guy friends) to be happy and popular. (Not sure where to start? Look for the perfume ads. Most of them show two people either half naked or making out. Also look for articles that teach you how to get, keep or understand a boyfriend.)

- **How many ads did you see that had a boyfriend and girlfriend looking blissfully happy staring into each other's eyes or frolicking down the beach hand in hand? Did you notice any articles that make it sound as though you *have* to have a boyfriend to be happy? Describe what you found and how it made you feel.**

In part 2, we'll talk a lot more about relationships and what it means to respect yourself while you're in (or not in) a relationship, so I won't go into it here. For now, I just want you to think about why we girls think we have to be in physical relationships to be happy.

- **Do you think others will respect you if you don't have a boyfriend? Do you think it's possible to have a boyfriend who respects you, even if you don't have a *physical* relationship with him?**

That devil's a sly character, but now that you've seen his obnoxious lies for what they are, I hope you'll expose his tricks every chance you get. He's got nothing on you if you refuse to believe his lies and instead trust in God's truth.

Psalm 101:2-3 (*NLT*) reads, "I will be careful to live a blameless life . . . I will lead a life of integrity in my own home. I will refuse to look at anything vile and vulgar. I hate all crooked dealings; I will have nothing to do with them." Now, I'm pretty sure the lies we've been talking about in this chapter fall under the category of "crooked dealings." Some of them might even fall under the category of "vile and vulgar." Either way, I think it's safest to have nothing to do with them. Would you agree?

We started this chapter with Philippians 4:8. Flip back a few pages and read it again, but this time insert the words "look at" every place you see "think about." (Go ahead, I'll wait.) Will you commit with me to look only at things that are true, honorable, pure and ultimately worth our time?

Let's pray.

> God, I've been blinded by Satan's lies through the media for too long. Open my eyes to see the truth about who I am and what will bring me true and lasting happiness. I know it's going to be hard, but show me the trash in my life that I need to get rid of so that I can focus on becoming a young woman of character and dignity. I love You. Amen.

Notes:

1. Angela Bole, "We Must Stop Glorifying Physical Beauty," *The Minnesota Daily Online*, December 9, 1999. http://www.mndaily.com/daily/1999/12/09/editorial_opinions/o21209/ (accessed October 11, 2004).
2. Dannah Gresh, *Secret Keeper* (Chicago, IL: Moody Press, 2002), p. 19.

three: in a boy's world

*Pay attention to my wisdom; listen carefully to my wise counsel. Then you will
learn to be discreet and will store up knowledge.*
Proverbs 5:1-2, *NLT*

Have you ever wondered what it would be like to be a guy for a day? I've always thought it would be interesting to find out what guys think about us girls. Aren't you curious? I mean, I know they think it's stupid that we always go to the bathroom in groups and that it takes us way too long to get ready in the morning, but what do they think about other things—such as the way we *dress*?

🗩 **Is there anything about guys that really confuses you? If you could ask a guy one question about guys in general and he had to tell you the truth, what would you ask?**

I was largely in the dark about the internal workings of guys' minds—until I got married (and I still only grasp a tiny percentage of what goes on in my honey's gray matter). Once we said "I do," I could ask my husband, Paco, *any* question I wanted to and he had to answer (or he'd be on his own to make dinner). So I started picking his brain and discovered some answers to age-old questions, such as Why do guys watch so many hours of sports on TV? and What are guys *really* afraid of?

Sorry, I can't tell you the answers to those questions; I wouldn't want to ruin the joy of discovery when *you* get married! But one answer is so important that I just have to let the cat out of the bag. One of the "secrets" that Paco revealed to me through many, many discussions is something that I was *completely* in the dark about when I was a teenager (so I'm guessing you're in the dark too). I was totally shocked by what he told me, and I count it my duty and privilege as a woman who has the inside track to a real (not to mention very good-looking) guy to divulge these secrets to all you girls out there who are dying to know.

I'm going to tell you how the way you dress affects guys.

Now, you have to promise me one thing before you go any further. This is privileged information that could be used in a completely wrong way. You have to promise me that once you understand the secrets of what certain articles of clothing do to a guy's mental capacity, you won't wear those things just to get some extra glances from that cute guy in algebra class. Deal? Okay, then here we go.

I spy with my little eye, something. . .

Guys are very visual creatures.

To help you understand what I mean, let me give you an example. It is a little personal, so I need you to keep this between you and me, okay? When I got married, I found out that my husband thought that every part of my body was beautiful in every way—even the parts that I thought were embarrassing. Now, based on what we've learned so far, this shouldn't surprise you. I'm a woman; he's a man—he's *supposed* to find me mysterious and appealing, right? But here's my point: Even though Paco is good-looking, to see him running around the house without any clothes on would do nothing for me (besides make me break out in laughter). That's not the way a girl's mind works. When I see him, I think of the way it would *feel* to have his strong arms around me—I desire to feel safe, cherished and loved. This is one of the fundamental differences between guys and girls: Guys are visual; girls are touch oriented (and generally more romantic).

If you're still not convinced, let me be blunt with you. There is a very good reason why men purchase the majority of porn magazines (lots of visual images of a woman's body) whereas women buy the majority of romance novels (stories of men making women feel loved). Satan knows how to tempt men and women based on what they ultimately desire—what "turns them on."

🗩 **If guys are more visual than girls, how might they see the ways girls dress differently from the way girls would?**

I remember hearing that a guy's eyes start where a girl's clothes end. For example, if I were to wear a knee-length jean skirt with a 6-inch slit, a guy's eyes wouldn't gravitate to my knees; they would naturally gravitate toward the top of the slit. Or if I were to wear a V-neck tee that revealed just a little cleavage, guess where his eyes would be drawn? It's a natural optic phenomenon, really.

But you don't have to take my word for it. I tracked down a few real, live guys to get their perspectives on the way girls dress.

GUYS SPEAK OUT

Wes, age 18
TJ, age 16
Trent, age 15

Q: How can the way a girl dresses affect a guy?

Wes: Well, it can give a positive or a negative impression, depending on the morals of the person who's looking. As a Christian, if a girl is wearing skimpy clothes, it can make a guy think impure thoughts, which isn't helpful to us Christian brothers. If she's actually covering her body, it makes us respect her.

TJ: If a girl walks into a room and she is wearing a very low-cut shirt and a short skirt, she will get a lot of attention from the guys in the room, but not good attention, because a lot of high school guys aren't thinking the best thoughts.

Trent: I am a very visual guy, and I am also a very imaginative guy. When a girl wears something revealing, it reminds me of everything I have seen girls wear in the past, or what they haven't worn. I would call it a "trigger." It attracts my sight, and in turn my imagination, which leads me down the path of fantasizing about that image. It triggers lust, which the Bible says is wrong.

Q: If you could give a shout to Christian girls about the way they dress, what would you tell them?

Wes: Well, my mom would say, "Don't wear anything you wouldn't feel comfortable wearing in front of Jesus." Ha ha. I'd say just cover yourselves better.

TJ: You don't have to dress like pop stars, movie stars and models—dressing skimpy isn't the best way to get a guy's attention. Respect yourselves. If I had a girlfriend, I wouldn't want her to dress skimpy.

Trent: I don't think there is anything wrong with trying to attract guys—you just have to be careful how you choose to attract them. Wearing revealing clothes will get you more looks from guys and more attention from guys. Guys will flirt with you more, and you will most likely feel better about yourself because of that. However, [you knew this was coming] it will be out of lust that the guy likes you. This causes the guy to sin. This causes me to sin.

Q: What types of clothes do girls wear that make it the hardest for you to keep your eyes looking at hers?

Wes: Short skirts and low-cut shirts definitely grab a guy's focus. Also, if you've got a thong popping out of your pants, that tends to attract one's eyes.

TJ: Clothes that make their breasts pop out, like V-necks and tube tops.

Trent: I am not into fashion, so my knowledge on this is limited. I think the girls themselves know better than any guy if they are trying to be revealing or not. As I said, revealing things are a trigger to a guy's mind; you have to have the wisdom to wear things that will set a guy's mind off the least amount. And you might even be as bold as to ask the guys whom you are around, "Do you think that what I am wearing is too revealing?" Most of us would probably say no, but the most honest might say yes, and then you'll know and have some guidelines.

Q: When a girl dresses sexy or to get attention, do you tend to respect her more or less?

Wes: Definitely less. Even if a non-Christian guy likes the skimpiness, he still won't respect her; he just wants to see what else she's willing to show.

TJ: I lose respect for her and feel bad for her because she feels that she has to stoop that low to get a guy's attention.

Trent: Always less. What she's wearing on the outside reveals some of her inner character, and it tells me that she may be desperate for attention. She might not be desperate, but that's the signal it sends.

Q: What makes you respect a girl the most?

Wes: Her personality and how she presents herself.

TJ: High self-esteem, good morals and when she is comfortable with herself.

Trent: A love for God and for people, independence and confidence. I respect any girl who has the guts to take off her mask.

> 💬 **What do you think about what these guys had to say? Did their answers surprise you? Do they make you want to change the way you dress?**

I GET NO REJPECT

I hear a lot of girls say that it's not their fault if a guy can't keep his eyes to himself. They say that if an outfit is cute, they have the right to wear it—guys are just going to have to learn to control their raging hormones.

💬 **Do you agree with that attitude? Why or why not?**

I'm not saying that guys don't have any responsibility, but I think they've been getting the bad rap for too long. You see, if you want to be respected by guys for who you are and what you have to offer on emotional and spiritual levels (rather than just physical), you need to do two things: (1) earn their respect, and (2) give them respect in return. That doesn't sound too unreasonable, does it? So let's talk about how we can do that.

To gain a guy's respect, you must first respect yourself. Then you must *show* him that you respect yourself by dressing in a way that encourages him to look you in the eyes instead of scanning you up and down.

- **What do you think it means to keep a guy looking you in the eyes? If that was your goal, what type of things would you *not* wear?**

The cool thing is that once you've mastered step 1 (earning guys' respect), you're automatically practicing step 2 (respecting guys in return). Let me explain. We've already learned that a guy struggles big-time with visual temptation. So what better compliment could you give him than to say, "You know what? I respect you so much that I'm going to give up my right to wear that 'cute' outfit because I know that it would be hard for you not to look at me in a degrading way." Now, *that's* dignity!

- **If girls showed guys respect by being more careful of what they wore, how do you think society would be different?**

- **Do you respect yourself and the guys around you enough to give up wearing any item of clothing that broadcasts your body, even if it's *super* cute? Why or why not?**

others can help

Speaking of "cute," we girls need to have a little chat. Imagine for a moment that you're at the mall with one of your best girlfriends looking for that perfect dress for homecoming. You've both got as many dresses as the attendant will let you have in your dressing rooms and you're just sure that you're going to find the perfect garb for the dance. You suddenly hear your friend exclaim from the adjacent stall, "Oh, I think this might be the one!" When you slip your head out of your door to get a peek, you see that your friend is wearing a dress that pushes her "chest" up and out so far that you're afraid she will fall completely out of her dress during the first conga line.

How would you respond to your friend in this situation?

a) Exclaim, "Oh, that *is* cute!"
b) Offer, "It's alright, but I'm not sure if that's your color."
c) Say as delicately as possible, "You look like you're going to fall completely out of your dress during the first conga line."
d) Say nothing and duck back into your dressing room.

The problem, girls, is that most of us in that situation would opt for (a). Here's why: We're so used to judging what's cute by what we see in magazines and on TV that we don't even *recognize* when an outfit crosses the line. Because we're not turned on visually as guys are, we see no problem with showing a few too many inches of cleavage or belly. But I guarantee that guys are noticing, and we girls aren't helping each other out when we ignore the obvious.

Now, because we're not visual, it can be difficult for us to tell whether an outfit would be a struggle for a guy. If you're not sure, *ask one*. A brother or dad (as opposed to your latest crush) would be an excellent candidate for such an inquiry.

God has put your dad in your life to protect your dignity. He's not out to be the "cute police," determined on keeping you from looking good. You may think he's old-fashioned, but guess what, *he's a man*; and as a man he has some pretty good insight into what will or won't mess with a guy's head. So listen to him. Plus, God tells us that we're to respect our parents' wishes (see Deuteronomy 5:16). So, if the parental units say an outfit is off-limits, don't fight them on it. Instead, thank your lucky stars that God has given you folks who respect you enough to tell you the truth and to encourage you to respect yourself.

- Have your parents given you guidelines for what you can and can't wear out of the house? How do you feel about those rules? After reading this chapter, do you understand their reasoning a little more?

- Would your friends tell you the truth if you wore something that didn't flatter your body type or that would turn guys on? Are you the type of person who would tell your friends the truth?

So now you know the secret behind a guy's visual nature. I hope that you'll think about these insights every morning as you pick out the day's attire. Remember, to get respect, you have to earn it and you have to show it. Do those two things and you'll be one dignified lady.

Let's pray.

> God, forgive me for not being aware of the way my clothes can cause guys to struggle with temptation. I want to be a young woman who respects herself and the people around her. Remind me through my friends and family members when I confuse looking cute with looking sexually appealing. I want to bring You glory in everything I wear. Amen.

four
R-E-S-P-E-C-T

And I want women to be modest in their appearance. They should wear decent and appropriate clothing and not draw attention to themselves by . . . [wearing] expensive clothes. For women who claim to be devoted to God should make themselves attractive by the good things they do.
1 Timothy 2:9-10, *NLT*

In Proverbs 31:10-31, King Lemuel recites an oracle (a fancy word for wise counsel) his mother taught him about the virtues of a godly girl. His mom was one insightful lady, and she wanted to make sure her son knew what to look for in a future wife. In verse 25, she describes this type of girl as being clothed with two qualities: strength and dignity.

● **Why do you think Lemuel's mom used the words "strength" and "dignity" to describe the way a godly girl dresses?**

● **Based on what we learned in the last chapter about the way guys' minds work, how can you be sure that the way you dress encourages guys to respect, admire and honor you for who you are?**

The way we dress plays a big part in our dignity because our clothes show the people around us whether we respect ourselves. *Now, hold your horses,* you might be thinking. *You're not supposed to judge a book by its cover. It's what's inside that counts.* Well, you're mostly right. God does care more about what's inside than what's outside. He told Samuel, "The LORD does not look at the things man looks at. Man looks at the outward appearance, but the LORD looks at the heart" (1 Samuel 16:7). But the problem is that only *God* can see our hearts. We have to rely on our limited five senses to determine what someone believes and values, which means we *do* tend to judge books by their covers. I mean, tell me the truth, if the cover of this book sported a picture of a frumpy, middle-aged mom wearing old-school clothes, would you even consider reading it? I rest my case.

> ● Check out this statement: "Usually what we wear on the outside reflects who we are on the inside." Do you agree? Why or why not?

If God cares most about what's inside but the people around us mostly see what's outside, what can we do to make sure that our friends (both guys and girls) get an accurate picture of the godly girls we really are? In other words, how can we be sure that we're sending the *right* messages by what we wear? I'm glad you asked! Here are a few tips I've learned over the years to help get you dressed for success.

avoid **dignity** killers

I truly believe that deep down, every girl longs to be respected by guys. Yet some girls dress in a way that screams, "All I've got is this body!"

There are a few sure-fire ways to send the absolute wrong messages to the people we come in contact with each day. The first step to making sure we're sending messages of respect is to avoid these dignity killers.

EXPOSED CREVICES

It used to be that seeing someone else's crack was a *bad* thing—it grossed us out. And just the *thought* of someone else seeing *your* cheeks exposed was enough to make a girl blush. It used to be that stories about exposing your bum were worthy of display in the "Most Embarrassing Moments" columns in magazines. Ah, but not in this age of liberation!

Today, you can show a bit of behind and actually be en vogue, according to a Roxy ad I found in a popular surf magazine. The page shows a cute gal in swimsuit bottoms and a tank with a big, floppy straw hat. Her torso is turned just enough so that both her rear end and her mug can face the camera. As she gives an "Oops, did I do that?" look, her thumbs tug her suit bottoms just enough to show about an inch more of her buttocks than I ever needed to see. Now, I don't know about you, but it just seems weird to me that Roxy wants girls across America to think that it's not only normal to show backside cleavage but also that it's *cute* to do so.

When I saw the Roxy ad, I was worried that maybe I was just out of sync with the times. I thought, *Maybe girls don't think it's a big deal to expose their butts to the world.* So I was relieved when I came across a particular Tampax® ad. It shows a girl in front of some lockers with her back to the camera. Apparently, her jeans were a bit too threadbare and—lo and behold—she has a three-inch rip down the seam of a back pocket. I'm not sure how she made it through the day without feeling the draft, but nevertheless, here's an exposed gal who's going to have to face her entire precalculus class after lunch. The heading above the picture says, "Do you tell her?"

Consider the irony here. Roxy wants us to believe that exposing ourselves for all to see is cute and even appealing. Tampax is banking on the fact that we'd be embarrassed as all get-out if we unexpectedly showed *any* part of our rear ends in front of our friends. So, as girls on a quest to develop dignity, which is it?

🗩 **Do you relate more with the Roxy ad or the Tampax ad? Do you think it's ever to your advantage to reveal this much skin to others?**

THONG THRONG

Just in case you're thinking, *Yeah, okay—I get it, but normal girls don't go around pulling their bathing suits down in front of cameras*, let's look at an even more common dignity killer (very similar to the first) that may shed some light on why I think these topics are so important to cover (no pun intended).

I recently went to a high school basketball game with my husband, Paco. We got there late, so we started the ascent to one of the nosebleed rows in the seemingly mile-high bleachers. After we had settled in and spotted the guy we had come to watch, I reached down to put my purse on the floor. Ugh! Not a foot from my face was a pink thong in all its glory, the owner in front of me completely oblivious that her Victoria's Secret was no longer a secret! I carefully sat back up, trying to quickly find something else to look at, but that was impossible to do—the entire row of girls in front of us had the same thing going on. They were all chatting away and watching the game, completely oblivious to the fact that the entire top three rows of the gym (mostly men—*old* men) were getting more than the price of admission should have covered.

- If you were in my shoes, what would you have done? Would it have bothered you to see a row of young women with their underwear exposed while you were trying to watch the game? What if your brother or boyfriend were sitting with you? Would you have said something to the thong throng?

I was embarrassed for these girls and for my husband, who was trying so hard not to look at the thong display in front of him. My only regret is that I didn't have an appropriate opportunity to talk to the girls about how wearing low-cut pants that expose their underwear to the world isn't necessarily a positive thing. Would you listen if someone told you that?

The bottom line—okay, that pun was on purpose—is that *underwear* is meant to be just that, so keep them hidden, even if that means you can't wear those superlow low-riders that your friend said are so cute on you.

Canyons of Cleavage

It's a fact of life that God has given some girls more on top than others, but whether your cup size is A or DD, He expects you to be responsible with what He's given you. Remember, *every* female body is beautiful, and we've already learned that beautiful female bodies have the ability to amaze our male counterparts.

Let's be real here. Those of you who are farther along in the alphabet will have a harder time finding shirts and tanks that will keep guys looking at you in the eyes than will those of you who are on the smaller side. But even though it's not your fault that your body is shaped the way it is, you are still held to the same guidelines for dignity as the girls who can get away with only a shelf bra in their tank tops. Just because your friends can wear a style doesn't mean you can (or should)!

I know it doesn't seem fair. In fact, this is an area I struggled with most of my life. I had an especially hard time when summer rolled around. Being a D cup, I had a horrific time trying to find a swimsuit that didn't make me look as though I belonged on a *Sports Illustrated* swimsuit calendar. It was *sooo* not fair that my friends could wear those cute little Roxy bikinis without fear of exposing themselves, whereas I was relegated to the misses section (boring!). It's still hard for me when I try on that adorable summer dress only to discover it turns my chest into the Grand Canyon, but I've learned (and am still learning) that it's best to wait and save my money for an outfit that flatters what God has given me while preserving the mystery of my body for my *husband*. I think you'll find that's a good principle to live by.

Based on your body type, what types of T-shirts, tanks or dresses are better left on the mannequin? Are you okay with leaving them there, or are you sometimes tempted to wear those tops, even though you know they might be borderline showy? Why do you think that is?

Muffin Tops

Imagine that you're at your favorite store with your friend Julia. You each grab a few outfits to try on and head to the dressing rooms. Julia's not overweight but not super skinny either—she's just an average girl. So when she tries on a tight, low-rider style of pants, the waistband squeezes the natural layer of fat around her hips, producing bulges the size of New Jersey above her rear end. You can see it as plain as day, especially because the top she's wearing is a few inches shy of covering her midsection. Do you say anything to her?

I see girls with this look all the time and it drives me nuts—not because I'm some old spinster afraid of guys drooling over their bare skin, but because I'm *embarrassed* for the girls wearing these outfits! Why in the world would a girl *want* to wear clothes that accentuate those features she spends most of her time complaining about? If a girl wants to be respected and admired, she has to choose outfits that show off her *best* features.

If you want to have dignity, choose clothes that fit your body type. Avoid jeans that give you "muffin tops," shorts that produce a continual wedgie, shirts that don't cover what should be covered and skirts that show off your undies every time you sit down. When you look in the mirror, don't ask if you can *get away* with your outfit. That's not the point! The goal is to have the outside match the inside, so show the world that you're a confident, godly gal by choosing practical, becoming and (of course) fashionable clothes.

Take a field trip to your closet. Spend a good 20 to 30 minutes giving yourself a fashion show. Try on as many outfits as you have time for. As you try on each outfit, decide whether it fits well, flatters your best features and would keep guys looking you in the eyes. Put any item that doesn't fit all three categories in a big plastic bag to donate to your favorite charity. When you're done with the assignment, write a short prayer to God in the following space. Tell Him why you're purging your closet and ask Him to bless you for doing what you know is right.

dress for the occasion

One of the things I love about living in Southern California is that I can grow vegetables in my garden nearly all year round. Call it a strange obsession, but I absolutely *love* getting dirty and sweaty among my tomato plants, sugar snap peas and a whole host of other scrumptious delights. The only thing I love to do on a Saturday as much as work in my garden is to lay out by the pool, so sometimes I try to get the best of both worlds. While I work on my garden, I get a jump start on my tan by donning my swimsuit and a pair of board shorts. I don't think most people would have a problem with that. I'm on my own property with no one but my husband around.

But what if I wore that same outfit to a job interview? I'd still be looking for a job, that's what! Why? Because what's appropriate in my garden or at the beach isn't appropriate in a professional environment. That's just the way it goes.

This principle applies to all areas of life. You wouldn't wear a prom dress to school or exercise clothes to church (and if you did, you'd probably get some uncomfortable stares). Wearing a bikini top to a luau dance at school isn't the same as wearing it at the beach. Every type of clothing is meant for an appropriate setting.

💬 **Can you think of a few other examples of outfits that are okay in one setting and not in another? What happens when we mix them up?**

💬 **How is wearing clothing appropriate for the setting an important part of dignity?**

choose your bait wisely

On one of our backpacking trips, Paco and I found ourselves at a bait shop in the little town of Stanley, Idaho (population: 95). An entire wall of the store was filled with glittery, gummy, furry fishing lures. As I looked for some bug repellant (the mosquitoes up there could swallow a small dog), I overheard a conversation between the store owner and a customer looking to catch a particular type of fish. I was amazed that out of the (literally) hundreds of fishing lures, the owner knew the *exact* lure that would entice the fish this guy wanted to catch.

So what does that have to do with clothes? Imagine that finding a future husband who will honor, respect and admire you is like fishing in an alpine lake. You know the type of guy you want to "catch"—now all you need to do is find the right bait (and have patience!).

💬 **What type of bait (aka clothes) do you think will attract a godly guy with rock-solid character? What type of clothes do you think would attract the *wrong* kind of guy?**

💬 **What kind of guy are you potentially attracting by the clothes you wear?**

Think Twice

God tells us to think carefully about everything we do, including the way that we dress. Haggai 1:5-6 says, "Now, this is what the Lord Almighty says: 'Give careful thought to your ways. . . . You put on clothes, but are not warm.'"

💬 **What do you think God means by putting on clothes yet not being warm?**

💬 **How can being deliberate about what you wear ensure that your heart matches the messages others receive?**

You may not purposely wear an outfit to make guys swoon, but that doesn't mean it's okay to wear it. When your heart is in the right place, you'll be careful and deliberate about each item of clothing that you wear.

A young woman with dignity guards the mystery that God has given her, not only for the sake of the young men around her, but also for her sake, because she has more self-respect than to seek attention by flaunting her body. With great beauty comes great responsibility, and *you* are beautiful.

I love the verses from the beginning of this session, 1 Timothy 2:9-10, because they put everything into perspective. Reading these verses reminds me that everything I put on my body should be decent, appropriate and sensible and that I shouldn't wear outfits that I know will get me the wrong kind of attention. Most important, these verses remind me that the most attractive accessory a godly girl can wear is a heart ready to do good. When my heart is right, it will show on the outside. Then I can take Jesus' words to heart, "Therefore I tell you, do not worry about your life, what you will eat or drink; or about your body, what you will wear. Is not life more important than food, and the body more important than clothes?" (Matthew 6:25). Let's pray.

> Awesome Savior, I want to wear clothes that reflect the beautiful things You are doing in my heart. Bring people into my life who will confront me when I draw attention to myself with the clothes I wear or when I wear things that don't encourage others to respect me for who I am inside. Most important, teach me how to be truly stunning by doing good things for others and choosing what is right. I love You. Amen.

five: Stand TALL

Let no one look down on your youthfulness, but rather in speech, conduct, love, faith and purity, show yourself an example of those who believe.
1 Timothy 4:12, *NASB*

Your clothes aren't the only thing that will make or break your dignity. People (parents included) will show you the respect they feel you deserve based on how you live your life. First Timothy 4:12 says that the words we speak and the way we act should be a good example for the people around us. What better way to earn others' respect than by being a living, breathing example of what Christ can do in a person's life?

Our hearts play a big part in whether we will act and speak like Jesus because, according to Him, what is in our hearts will dictate our actions. In Luke 6:45, Jesus said, "The good man brings good things out of the good stored up in his heart, and the evil man brings evil things out of the evil stored up in his heart. For out of the overflow of his heart his mouth speaks."

● **List a few people you know personally whom you respect. Why do they deserve your respect? What did they do to earn it?**

● **Based *only* on the things you do and say (meaning your thoughts and feelings don't count for this question), do you think you deserve your friends' respect? How about your parents' respect? Why?**

The Bible says "a kindhearted woman gains respect" (Proverbs 11:16), so if we want to earn the respect and admiration of others, we should show the good that we have stored up in our hearts. We'll spend the rest of this chapter exploring some ways we can make sure our words and actions earn the respect we deserve.

YOU DON'T SAY

Let your speech always be with grace, as though seasoned with salt, so that you will know how you should respond to each person (Colossians 4:6, *NASB*).

Picture this: You're chilling at your casa with a group of friends, playing cards and laughing about the way your PE teacher snorts when he calls roll. The front door unexpectedly opens, and a really cute girl that you've never seen before walks into the room with another one of your friends. Can you see the heads turn? The girls in the room immediately wonder who this chick is and what she thinks she's doing crashing the party. Your guy friends also wonder who she is—and whether they can find a good reason to talk to her! Being the confident girl you are (and because it's your house), you introduce yourself and ask her whether she'd like to join your game of Go Fish. She opens her lovely mouth to answer and out flies enough vulgarity to make a sailor blush. Ouch! Her reply completely shatters her picture-perfect appeal.

● **Have you ever met someone (guy or girl) who you thought was really cute until you got to know him or her? What clues revealed that the inside didn't match the outside?**

● **Do you struggle with any of these speech "impairments"? Put a check mark next to any that apply to you.**

- ☐ Complaining
- ☐ Criticizing
- ☐ Cussing
- ☐ Disrespecting authority
- ☐ Flirting
- ☐ Gossiping

- ☐ Laughing at off-color humor
- ☐ Putting others down
- ☐ Using lots of sarcasm
- ☐ Telling dirty jokes
- ☐ Other:

TIP: If you're not sure whether you struggle with any of these bad speech habits, keep a log of everything you say for a day. If you have a tape recorder, with your friends' permission you could record conversations you have and then listen to them later. Either way, you may be surprised at what slipped through those lips of yours!

Most girls don't give much thought to the way they talk when they're with friends. It's especially easy to get caught up in any of the bad habits in this list when the people around you talk that way all the time.

● **Do your friends encourage you to speak with grace (see Colossians 4:6) or do they drag your mouth into the gutter?**

● **First Corinthians 15:33 reads, "Do not be misled: 'Bad company corrupts good character.'" What should you do if your friends drag you down and keep you from reflecting Christ in the words you speak?**

King David knew what it felt like to struggle with his speech. That's why he prayed, "May the words of my mouth . . . be pleasing in your sight, O Lᴏʀᴅ" (Psalm 19:14). If you struggle to keep your tongue under control, try posting this verse on a binder or somewhere else that you'll see it often. James 3 is also excellent reading if you're serious about taming that tongue of yours (careful, that chapter is not for the faint of heart!).

monkey see, monkey do

Obey God because you are his children. Don't slip back into your old ways of doing evil; you didn't know any better then. But now you must be holy in everything you do, just as God—who chose you to be his children—is holy (1 Peter 1:14-15, *NLT*).

Now that we understand how our words can encourage others to respect us, we shouldn't have too hard a time understanding that our conduct—the way we act—can also make or break our dignity.

First Peter 1:15 says that we're supposed to be holy (which means "set apart" or different from the world) in *everything* we do. Some Christians think that as long as they're not doing drugs, having sex or getting into serious trouble, they're in the clear. But I'm going to go out on a limb here and say that when Peter said "everything," he literally meant *everything*.

Just for fun, let's play a game of "Do You Ever." Here's how it works: I'm going to ask you a few questions about things that Christian teens sometimes do without thinking about the consequences. You put a check mark next to each question that reflects what you do on a regular basis. Make sense? Okay, here we go.

Do You Ever . . .

- ☐ Cheat on your homework or on tests?
- ☐ Do something physical with a guy that you would be ashamed to tell your parents about?
- ☐ Hurt your body on purpose (like cutting or starving yourself)?
- ☐ Listen to music with lyrics that you would be embarrassed to speak out loud?
- ☐ Take things that aren't yours?
- ☐ Watch movies that you are *really* glad your parents aren't with you to watch?

🗩 **How could these activities affect the level of respect you have for yourself? How about the level of respect others have for you?**

Go back and read 1 Peter 1:15 again. This verse calls us to grow up, to take a stand and to respect ourselves. Before Christ changed our lives, we did stupid things and didn't know any better. But now that we know what Christ did for us and understand the importance of being different from the world around us, we have no excuse. Now, God calls us to a higher standard.

🗩 **Write a prayer to God and talk to Him about the struggles you checked. Ask Him for the strength to be holy in *everything* you do and to bring you friends who will encourage you to do what's right.**

God says that He will always provide us a way out of every temptation (see 1 Corinthians 10:13), but we have to do our part and get out of Dodge when we know we're in a compromising situation.

💬 **Are there any places, people or situations that you know keep you trapped in a cycle of undignified behavior? What can you do to free yourself from those weights so that you can stand tall?**

ACTIONS SPEAK

Body language would fall under the "conduct" category, but this topic is so important that I'm going to give it a space all its own. A girl's stance, posture, facial expressions and all-around demeanor say a lot about who she is and what she stands for.

For example, I'm a notorious sloucher. I hate it—I really do—but unless I'm consciously thinking about sitting or standing up straight, I look like I just rolled out of bed and can barely stay awake. Now, that may not seem like a big deal, but when I'm talking to someone and it looks like I'm bored out of my skull—well, that doesn't do much for that person's self-esteem! So I'm working on straightening up and looking interested.

There are even louder, more damaging messages we can send with our bodies with frighteningly little effort on our parts. Pull out the magazine you used in chapter 2, or a similar magazine. We're going to do a little assignment.

💬 **Flip through your magazine and choose three ads (you can cut them out or mark the pages with tape) that use a model. In the space below, briefly describe each ad and then express what message you think the model's posture is sending readers like you. I'll give you one of mine to get you started.**

Jessie's Ad—Nicole Richie for Bongo® Jeans. She's kneeling on a bed, sticking her chest and rear out at the same time while biting on her necklace. It looks like she's trying to seduce some guy behind the camera. I'm hearing, "Come and get me!"

Ad 1—

Ad 2—

Ad 3—

💬 Many times the way we carry ourselves says more than our words do. Watch the girls around you the next time you're with a group of people, and then think about the way *you* carry yourself when you're with others. Write about what you find in the following space.

you are all-around beautiful

It would be better if they had never known the right way to live than to know it and then reject the holy commandments that were given to them (2 Peter 2:21, *NLT*).

Now we know that the things we say and do have as much—if not more—to do with beauty and dignity as the way we dress. Second Peter 2:21 reminds us that once we know the truth, we're responsible to live by it. So help preserve the beautiful allure that God has given you by acting and speaking in ways that make you even *more* beautiful to others than you already are. Let's pray.

God, I know that You've given me guidelines for living, not because You don't want me to have any fun, but because You want me to enjoy life as much as I possibly can. Forgive me for not acting and speaking like the lady I am. I want to be a beautiful reflection of Your Son in every area of my life. Amen.

six: fashion frenzy

I delight greatly in the Lord; my soul rejoices in my God. For he has clothed me with garments of salvation and arrayed me in a robe of righteousness . . . as a bride adorns herself with her jewels.

Isaiah 61:10

Maybe it's because my mom was an interior design major, but I've always had a thing for home decorating. My husband thinks I'm nuts (and you might too) because I keep a binder filled with clippings, ads and articles that contain ideas for my *dream* house (just in case I ever win the lottery, which is tough to do when you don't play). I've collected fabric samples, furniture ideas, cabinet designs, pictures of bedding, floor plans and about a hundred paint colors. I know, if you didn't think I was crazy before, you do now! But I do have a reason for exposing to you this peculiar quirk of mine.

When I first started developing a liking for all of this design stuff, I subscribed to *Better Homes and Gardens* magazine. Oh, I was in heaven! Each month I flipped through loads of pictures, and every room and every garden that the magazine highlighted was *perfect*. I just knew that if I could get a couple of the pieces of furniture that I saw on those pages, *my* living room would also be perfect.

So Paco and I saved up and bought our first set of real furniture (until then the pieces we owned were hand-me-downs or garage sale finds). All my dreams had come true. I was elated—until we got each piece situated in our living room. Something just wasn't right. It seemed that our living room was much smaller than the one in the picture; our new armoire didn't seem to glow as it was supposed to and the pillows on our couch didn't seem as plump as they should have been. Okay, my living room didn't look *anything* like the picture, even though we had practically the same pieces of furniture! It took me weeks to recover from the disappointment.

I learned an important lesson that day. With the right light, filters, fresh-cut flowers and budget, a good photographer could make my grandfather's musty La-Z-Boy look like a vintage piece of art. That's their job—to take ordinary objects and make them look so appealing in print that we just can't live without them.

- Do you think clothing designers do the same thing on TV, in the movies and in magazine ads?

- Have you ever seen an outfit on TV or in a magazine that you just *had* to have, but once you tried it on, you didn't feel the magic you expected? Describe your experience.

THE TRENDSETTERS

A few months ago, I saw an ad for an adorable black and white silk strapless dress. It looked pretty on the model and didn't show any cleavage, so I decided that if I ever came across one (for one-third the price this company wanted for it), I just might have myself a new outfit. To my surprise, the dress went on sale a few weeks later—for one-third the original price. Considering it fate, I ordered the dress and checked the mail every day for the next two weeks. The much-anticipated package came just in time for Valentine's Day, so the first time I wore my new dress was on a date with my husband.

Things went well at first (such as while I was putting on my makeup), but once we left the house, I discovered that the silky material in the dress had a way of sliding right down my body! I spent most of the night tugging at the top of the dress, trying to keep fabric where fabric belonged. Instead of remembering that night as a romantic date, I remember the tug-of-war I had with that oh-so-cute-on-paper dress.

I'm not alone, you know. I see girls all the time who are afraid to sit down because they know they don't have enough skirt to cover themselves when they do this strenuous of an activity, or who are constantly fiddling with their bra straps to keep the darn things under their tanks, or who have to remove a wedgie every few minutes because their shorts are too short. Ah, the price we pay for fashion.

- Can you relate to these impractical fashions? Do you feel that the clothes you wear not only fit your body but also fit your *lifestyle*? Or do you spend a considerable amount of time worrying that something is showing that shouldn't be showing?

Wearing clothes should not be difficult. It is indeed possible to find clothes that stay put so that you can be the fun, mobile person you are!

- Why do you think stores sell clothes that aren't practical for moving around in? Do you think there's a link between what stores sell and what designers print in magazines and show on TV?

- What do you think would happen if girls like us stopped buying clothes that were more trouble than they're worth?

the perfect fit

Call me crazy, but I think looking cute is a *good* thing. I'm all for fashion and style, and I'm also for finding outfits that work *for* me—not against me—during the day. I know it's possible to have the best of both worlds; I've been pretty successful at it (aside from my slippery dress incident!). The key is to be patient and to say no to the clothes that are cute but not quite good enough.

I know you'll feel great about yourself and will earn the respect of others when you master this fine art of shopping, so I'm going to go with you to some of your favorite stores and help you get started. But before we head out the door, here are a few tips I've found that will help you find the perfect outfits every time.

- When you're trying on a piece of clothing, don't just do a compact turn in front of the mirror. Move around a bit—as you would in real life—to see whether it's practical. Try sitting, bending over, or putting your hair in a ponytail. If you run into any of the dignity killers that we talked about in chapter 4, you'll know that the outfit is best left on the hanger.

- Listen to your own advice in the changing room. No joke—the following are some of the comments I heard from a group of girls the last time I went shopping (I didn't mean to eavesdrop, but they were talking really loud!):

  "Ugh, these shorts give me a big ol' wedgie."

  "My mom would flip if she saw me in this, but who cares, right?"

  "These pants make me look fat."

  If you hear yourself making comments like these, try, try again!

- If you're not sure if something fits right or looks good on you, ask a friend or parent for his or her honest opinion. (And don't be offended when they tell you the truth!)
- Stay within your budget. Just because you find something that fits your style and your body doesn't mean you should have to hand over your wallet or get a summer job to pay for your new clothes.

All right, now that we know what we're looking for, let's hit the mall. Seriously—this isn't like an extra-credit question on a history test that you don't have to answer if you get the others right. Grab a couple of friends and spend an hour or two browsing your favorite shops. In each store, find at least one outfit you want to try on. I've put together a little questionnaire for you to fill out while you're in the dressing room (or afterward if there's a long line of people waiting for a room). Don't worry, I'm going too. I'll fill out mine when I get there. But before we head out the door, let's pray.

Creative Father, You are the author of design and style! I know my affinity for fashion and style are a good thing, but I need Your help to make sure that my sense of style always reflects You. Thank You for teaching me what it means to live with dignity and self-respect in the things I wear and in the ways I act. I love You. Amen.

Store

PacSun

Jessie's Fashion Critique

Description of Outfit

White eyelet lace skirt with a brown tank top and multi-color ribbon belt.

Prices

Skirt: $29.50
Tank: $22.50
Belt: $19.50

Pros

I really like the fabric on the skirt—it's feminine but not too girly.

The brown tank is a good color with my skin and covers my chest, even when I bend over.

The belt is colorful—very unique.

Cons

When I sit down, I feel like I'm flashing the world because the skirt is so short! I can just see it creeping up on me. Not practical for wearing anywhere other than the dressing room.

The belt's a little too pricey for my budget.

What My Friends/Parents Think

Paco says he likes the tank a lot, but confirms my suspicions about the skirt. He says that my long legs just make it look even shorter.

Thumbs Up or Down?

Skirt—Two thumbs down
Tank—We have a winner!
Belt—One thumb down

Store

Description of Outfit

Prices

Pros

Cons

What My Friends/Parents Think

Thumbs Up or Down?

Store

Description of Outfit

Prices

Pros

Cons

What My Friends/Parents Think

Thumbs Up or Down?

Store

Description of Outfit

Prices

Pros

Cons

What My Friends/Parents Think

Thumbs Up or Down?

PART TWO:
Respect Your Heart—
learning to love
with dignity

seven: blue skies ahead

Every good and perfect gift is from above, coming down from the Father of the heavenly lights, who does not change like shifting shadows.

James 1:17

When I was a little girl, I loved playing with Barbie dolls. I would spend hours dressing the little dolls, taking them shopping, pretending they were headed to some important job or were taking an adventure to some far-off place (such as the neighboring town—everything seems far away in a five-year-old's world!). But my make-believe world changed the day that I got one of Barbie's friends for my birthday. Suddenly, just playing with Barbie's hair wasn't fun anymore. Now, all the make-believe games revolved around the new kid on the block—yup, good ol' Ken! I was transported to a different world, a world in which there were *boys*. Ken took Barbie on dates, they got married, and of course, they lived happily ever after—over and over again.

You may not have been a big Barbie fan when you were a kid, but I bet you watched Disney movies such as *Snow White and the Seven Dwarfs, Cinderella* and my personal favorite, *Sleeping Beauty*. Why do young girls love movies like those? Because girls—no matter how young—love tales of handsome princes, romance and dreams coming true. And at that age, a girl still respects herself enough to think that she *deserves* Prince Charming.

> **What sort of make-believe games did you play as a young girl? Did you have dreams of Prince Charming coming to rescue you someday? (Go ahead—let your mind relive some of those early dreams of love!)**

We never really grow out of those dreams of romance. Oh, we may grow a little (okay, a lot) calloused when we discover that sometimes members of the opposite sex don't think we're as dreamy as *we* think we are or when we watch the pain divorce causes, but somewhere deep down we may still crave a match made in heaven.

💬 **What sort of dreams do you have today about romance and your future husband? How are they similar to the dreams you had as a child? How are they different? What do you think caused you to change your dreams? (Take about 5 to 10 minutes so that you can really think through your answers.)**

a match made
in heaven

Did you know that God is the author of love, romance and marriage? Seriously, He made them! There's no way it was our idea—we humans just couldn't come up with such heavenly imaginings all on our own.

The Bible says, "God *is* love" (1 John 4:16, emphasis added). He is the very *definition* of that thing we crave so much. That leads me to believe that He must have the inside scoop on what works and what doesn't work in our pursuit to find true love. James 1:17 says that God is also the giver of every perfect gift. (I'm pretty sure finding and marrying the man of your dreams would fall under that category.) Now, here's the best part—God *wants* to give you a match made (literally) in heaven! How do I know? I just text-messaged Him and He told me. Not really, but He does tell us in His Word (over and over) that He wants us to experience the best life has to offer (see Jeremiah 29:11, John 10:10 and Romans 12:2).

So if God knows all about love, is the only One who can give us the awesome gift of finding true love, *and* wants us to experience the best life has to offer, wouldn't you say that we had better entrust our hearts to Him?

💬 **Have you ever specifically asked God to take control of your dreams of true love? If not, take a few minutes to do that now.**

If God's plans for you include marriage, He wants to handpick the perfect man for you. He wants you to enjoy the fulfillment, joy, peace and fun that such a relationship can bring, and He doesn't want you to have to go through years of rejection, guilt and broken dreams to get there. That's why He gives us some guidelines for relationships. It should come as no surprise that these guidelines are synonymous with dignity. In other words, God's ideas about relationships and having self-respect go hand in hand.

JUNGLE BALL

Let's review: Since God knows all about love, is the giver of true love, and wants us to experience the best life has to offer, we can trust that His guidelines for relationships will help us get closer to our dreams.

If you're like me, everything sounded great until you got to the part about "guidelines." You might be thinking, *Rules for love? That sounds really boring. Doesn't God know that love has to do its own thing?* But don't chuck this book just yet—let me explain what I mean when I say that those guidelines will help us get closer to our dreams.

I played several sports in high school, but volleyball was my favorite (if you're not a volleyball fan, just humor me). Imagine with me for a second that there are no rules in volleyball. You can hit the ball as many times as you want before sending it back over (or under) the net, it doesn't matter where the ball goes and no one keeps score. Talk about jungle ball! I would have hated playing. The rules that make up the game of volleyball actually make it *fun*—they help us enjoy the game.

You can probably see where I'm going with this. The guidelines, or rules, that God gives us to govern relationships actually make the dating process more enjoyable. It wasn't hard for me to follow the rules in volleyball because I knew they were an important part of the game. I wish I had known the same about the dating game!

💬 **Do you think it sounds reasonable or unreasonable that God would give us guidelines for relationships? Whether or not you think it's fair of God to give us guidelines, how might having rules in the world of dating actually help us enjoy the "game" more?**

THE GOLD MEDAL

My friend Shelly (Stokes) VanHouwelingen played catcher for the 1996 USA Olympic softball team that won the gold medal that year. This woman puts the A in "athlete," folks. Shelly not only has athleticism oozing out of her pores, but she also knows what it means to represent her homeland on and off the field. When an athlete is chosen to represent the United States in an international competition, such as the Olympics, it is important to make sure that he or she won't embarrass us before or after the event. Olympic athletes are called to a higher standard than the rest of us because they can make our country either look good or ridiculous in front of the world. Lucky for us Americans, Shelly is a godly woman who makes us look *good*!

Being part of God's family is a bit like being on an Olympic team. The rest of the world is watching us to see whether this "Jesus thing" is worth a hill of beans. Often the only way they will see Christ is through the way *we* represent Him. Scary, huh? That's why God expects His "athletes" to make Him proud in every area of their lives—including in the quest for love. Part of having dignity is accepting the fact that our Coach is counting on us to follow the rules and be a good example of godliness to all the people who are watching. Are you up for the challenge?

💬 **If you could be an Olympic athlete in any sport, which sport would you choose? What do you think would be the hardest part of representing your country?**

💬 **What is the hardest part of representing God in the way you live your life? Is that struggle worth winning the gold?**

Pearly Whites

Strength and dignity are her clothing, and she smiles at the future (Proverbs 31:25, *NASB*).

Does this verse sound familiar? It was the very first verse we read in chapter 1. Notice the words "she smiles at the future." Why do you think she's showing off those pearly whites? If you hold yourself with dignity and dress and act in ways that demand respect, you too can smile when you think of the future because you can be confident that if having a husband is what's best for you, God will bring you a man who loves you for the right reasons.

💬 **For review, what role does the way we dress play in attracting a godly guy? (Hint: think fishing lure!) What roles do the ways that we act and speak play?**

The guidelines that God has for our relationships basically boil down to three main ideas: (1) honor God, (2) have respect for yourself, and (3) have respect for your future husband. We'll spend the next five chapters talking about practical ways that we can be successful in our quest for love while preserving our hearts for the good gift God has in store for us. Let's pray.

> Loving God, thank You for creating romance and marriage to meet the needs for intimacy that You have given us. I trust that since these were Your ideas, You also know the best way to play the game. Teach me Your rules for relationships not only so that I represent You well, but also so that I can have a fulfilling life in the process. In Jesus' name, amen.

my space

Above all else, guard your heart, for it is the wellspring of life.
Proverbs 4:23

In junior high, I had a new crush every two weeks. I wish I were joking. Like clockwork, I would see some guy at school (who maybe smiled at me at just the right time) and I was smitten. Of course, I hardly ever *talked* to any of these guys, let alone got any feedback whatsoever from them that they were interested in me. Nevertheless, I spent countless hours devising clever plans to end up next to them in line for lunch and thinking about what I would say if they did happen to notice that I existed.

💬 **Whether you're in junior high or high school, can you relate to my dilemma? Write about the results of your crushes.**

But that's pretty harmless, right? I mean, all junior high and high school girls flit from crush to crush, letting their whole worlds revolve around guys they hardly know—but then in college they find "the one" and live happily ever after. That's what I thought anyway. But when I got to college, the cycle continued. The crushes lasted a little longer (such as two months), but my love life felt more like reruns of *The Twilight Zone* than the dreams of romance that I had as a kid playing with my Barbie dolls. Crushes and relationships with guys became a type of addiction for me. I constantly had to have an interest in a guy, whether or not he returned my attention. Unfortunately, I didn't realize how much damage I was doing to my heart.

💬 **Do you consider your crushes harmless? Why or why not?**

keeping your heart whole

In Proverbs 4:23, Solomon (who happened to be the wisest man who ever lived) said, "Above all else, guard your heart, for it is the wellspring of life." More than money, possessions and even your physical body, Solomon says that you should guard the center of your emotions. Hmmm . . .

💬 **Why do you think Solomon was so concerned that we guard our hearts? What could damage them? What happens when they are damaged?**

I wish someone would have told me when I had my first crush the value of guarding my heart. If I would have been more careful to keep my emotions in check, I wouldn't have had my heart broken 236 times. (I wish this were an exaggeration!) If I would have been more protective of the "wellspring of [my] life," I would have been able to experience so much more of what life had to offer. Let me explain.

learning from a water balloon

If you have a balloon nearby, fill it with water and tie it off (don't give in to the temptation to throw it at your little brother). If you don't have one handy, just play along. Get a small needle and poke a small hole in the bottom half of the balloon (be sure to do this part over a sink). Instead of bursting, the pinprick should start a slow leak of water. Gently poke a few more holes around the base of the balloon. The balloon will soon start shrinking as more and more water slowly drips out. If you watch it long enough, all of the water in the balloon will eventually leak out.

Here's the point: The water balloon represents your heart. Every unassuming pinprick represents a crush, a relationship—any emotional involvement that gives away a small piece of your heart. With enough pinpricks and with enough time, your wellspring will be out of water. The fewer the pinpricks, the more of your heart you will have to present to your future husband.

💬 How would you feel if, when God finally introduced you to the man He has been saving and preparing for you, you didn't have any water left in your balloon to give him?

💬 How would you feel if you had been guarding your balloon from pinpricks, but his balloon was completely empty?

having a
pure heart

Create in me a pure heart, O God (Psalm 51:10).

The Bible talks quite a bit about having a pure heart, but what does that mean? Glad you asked. My favorite definition of "pure" comes from *Webster's Dictionary.*

pure (pyur) adj–containing nothing that does not properly belong[1]

Pretty simple, huh? Pure gold doesn't have aluminum in it, pure water doesn't have little brown floaties in it, and a pure heart doesn't get weighed down by feelings for guys that don't belong there. Having a pure heart is all about protecting it from emotions that distract you from whom truly belongs there—God and, one day, your husband.

If you have self-respect and dignity, instead of giving your heart away to every cute guy who crosses your path, you will keep your feelings in check. Giving your heart away to any guy who is interested (and especially to those who *aren't* interested) shows a lack of self-respect for yourself and a lack of respect for your future husband. Falling for guys willy-nilly cheapens true romance. Instead of something to wait for and look forward to, love becomes a worn-out pair of shoes—you can always find another pair.

💬 Would you describe your heart as pure right now? What feelings is your heart holding on to that don't belong there? (Not just feelings for guys—include anger, jealousy, hate and so on.)

💬 Are you willing to do a little spring cleaning in your heart? What can you do to start clearing out the harmful feelings to make room for the one who truly belongs there?

PURSUING GUYS

When I look back at the many crushes I've had in my life, a sad truth smacks me in the face. Most of the time, the guy that I thought would make my dreams come true didn't give me the time of day. I'm a bit embarrassed to admit it—the only reason I'm humiliating myself by revealing this secret is because I have a sneaking suspicion you might be able to relate. Most of the time, we girls are so blinded by feelings of infatuation that we sacrifice our interests, our friends, our thoughts, our time and even our bodies for guys who don't respect or value us the way we deserve to be cherished. What's that all about? Why do intelligent, beautiful, got-it-goin'-on girls pawn away their time and energy on guys who don't give a rip about them? When are we going to get a clue and have a little dignity? Ladies, please, please, please make the guy pursue *you*. Make him prove that he values you enough to seek you like the treasure you are.

I'm going to let you in on another little secret that I've learned since I've been married. God designed guys to pursue us, not the other way around. If you make it obvious to a guy that you're head over heels for him (such as by flirting, sending him excessive text messages or e-mails, telling your friends to "accidentally" mention that you like him), a quality guy is going to back off big-time. A guy isn't forced to respect and honor a girl who fawns over him, because he doesn't have to work for her affection.

💬 Okay, let's be honest with each other. On a scale of 1 to 10, do you tend to pursue guys or make them do the pursuing?

1   2   3   4   5   6   7   8   9   10

I make guys pursue me.   I go after guys that I like.

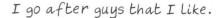

💬 **Give some examples that support the rating you chose.**

I was so impatient and headstrong as a teenager that I ended up scaring off most of the guys that I was interested in. It took me a long time to figure out that I needed to have more self-respect and wait for a guy who would think, *Wow, that Jessie is something else. I think I want to get to know her better.* Once I focused on keeping my heart pure and stopped chasing boys, God did in fact bring me the man of my dreams—a man who respects, values and pursues me.

💬 **Are you willing to wait patiently for a man who appreciates all that you are? Write a short prayer, asking God to help you focus on keeping your heart pure until that time.**

respecting your space

Having boundaries in your life is a good thing. They're like No Trespassing signs that warn unauthorized people not to step foot onto private property. Our personal boundaries keep intruders out and also keep us from giving too much of ourselves to others.

💬 **What are some examples of good boundaries?**

Emotional boundaries are a healthy part of making sure that we don't give away our hearts too soon. Here's the trick: It's best to define what those boundaries are *before* you're in a relationship with a guy. (Our minds have a way of getting muddled when we're all ga-ga, you know what I mean?) So let's take some time now to figure out the emotional boundaries that are right for you. I've jotted down some questions to get you thinking. Use the space provided to write down specific boundaries for yourself.

Questions to Ponder

- How will you know if you're starting to pursue a guy instead of letting him pursue you? What will you do if that happens?
- How much time will you spend talking on the phone with a guy you like?
- Will you e-mail and text-message him? How often?
- Will you spend time alone with him, or will you only hang out in groups?
- How will you respond if a guy expresses interest in you? Will you automatically show interest back, or will you continue to guard your heart? Why?
- Based on your experience with guys, what other boundaries would be healthy for you to put up in your heart?

My Personal Boundaries

> Dear Father, I want to save my whole heart for You and for the man with whom I will spend my life. Teach me how to have healthy emotional boundaries so that I can preserve my dignity and stop giving my heart away. I want my heart to be pure for You, Lord. Amen.

Note:

1. *Merriam-Webster's Collegiate Dictionary,* 11th ed., s.v. "pure."

nine: just dreamy!

Whatever is true, whatever is noble, whatever is right, whatever is pure,
whatever is lovely, whatever is admirable—if anything is excellent or praiseworthy—
think about such things. . . And the God of peace will be with you.
Philippians 4:8-9

Did you know that the emotions we feel actually stem from our thoughts? Let's do an experiment. Imagine you're on a beautiful island in the South Pacific, walking along the beach and letting the warm, salty water cover your toes. What feelings do these thoughts spark? I feel totally relaxed yet slightly restless, because these thoughts make me want to *go* to the South Pacific, not just think about it! Now think about your best friend moving away or that math test you failed last week. How do you feel now? Sad? Frustrated? Angry?

The human mind is a tricky arena—especially the *female* mind! We girls can create entire make-believe worlds in the hidden rooms of our minds at the drop of a hat. As innocent as our experiment was, the implications in the world of romance are a bit scary. If we don't control the thoughts we have about guys and romance, we won't be able to control our emotions either. Let me give you yet another embarrassing example from my own life.

It was just another regular Sunday in my home town of Frazier Park, California. I arrived at youth group that evening with no expectations for anything out of the ordinary. I found a couple of friends and we took our seats. Then, as if in a dream, I watched a guy that I had never seen before grab his guitar and start to lead us in worship. "Who's that?" I whispered to my friend. "Oh, he's the youth pastor's nephew, visiting from some town at the beach," she whispered back. And then it happened: Like an uncontrollable flood, thoughts poured through my head the entire time he led worship. The thoughts went something like this:

Oh, wow. I think he's the cutest guy I've ever seen! And he sounds so godly leading worship. I wonder how long he's staying in town. Maybe he'll stick around after the meeting for refreshments and I could introduce myself. What would I say? Will he like me? What if he liked me so much that he decided to come to our youth group every week? Oh, that would be the coolest! What if . . . he's THE ONE? I could totally see myself marrying a godly, cute guy like him. I bet he would want to stay at the beach—I've always wanted to live at the beach. He could be a worship pastor—and our kids would be so cute. I bet he would make a great dad, and I would make him so happy.

And so it went. By the end of the third song I was completely smitten for this guy I had never even *met!* I didn't even know his name yet.

Well, it turned out that he didn't fall head over heels for me. Although he really was a cool guy, he only came to the youth group once or twice after that, and my make-believe world came crashing down all around me.

● Can you relate to my story? Have you ever found yourself daydreaming about a guy or a relationship that you wish you had? What feelings accompanied those daydreams?

● Can you see any potential dangers in letting your mind wander wherever it pleases? What kind of boundaries in your thought life would help you avoid those dangers?

Since our emotions start with our thoughts, we have to be very careful about what and about whom we choose to think. The apostle Paul knew how important thoughts are. That's why he encouraged the Philippians to think about things that are true (which eliminates make-believe worlds like the one I made up in youth group that night), pure, lovely and worthy of praise (see Philippians 4:8-9). When we choose to take control of our thoughts and think only about things that encourage us to save our hearts for God and for our future husbands, Paul says that our hearts will be filled with *peace*—an emotion we all want, right?

wild thoughts

Unfortunately, thinking about things that are true, pure, lovely and worthy of praise doesn't come naturally. Our thoughts are a bit like unruly wild animals that don't want to stay in their cages. And just like wild animals, some thoughts appear perfectly harmless at first glance—until you get too close!

> 💬 **How do you think we can tame our wild thoughts while encouraging good thoughts to grow stronger? Give some specific examples.**

We've all heard the phrase "what goes in comes out." I think this especially applies to our thought life. Whatever we let into our minds will shape our thoughts. For example, if I were to watch a scary movie (which I never do because they freak me out), I would spend the rest of the night thinking about people hiding in my car or coming after me in a dark alley. If I were to watch a romantic chick flick, I'd spend the rest of the night wishing that Paco were more romantic (which would be totally unfair to him, because he *is* romantic! Sad, huh?). The same is true of TV shows, books and especially music.

> 💬 **What types of music to you like to listen to? What bands or artists are your favorites? What specific songs rock your world?**

The music we listen to has a profound affect on our thoughts and, thus, on our emotions. I know, I know, you don't listen to the words, right? You just like the beat. Well, even if I did believe you, different types of instrumental songs can shape our thoughts too. That's why I play George Winston (instrumental piano) when I'm trying to wind down for the night or when I want to feel smart, and I play Latin jazz (now there's a beat!) when I want to get things done around the house or when I want to pretend I can dance. Rap (even without the words) tends to make us think one type of thought and heavy metal tends to make us think another.

But what if song lyrics really *do* affect us? If we're honest with ourselves, we know they do. (How could we know every word to a song and not be affected?) To this day, when I hear certain songs, they take me back to unhealthy thoughts and relationships that I had years ago. That's scary! If we want to keep our hearts pure—containing only who belongs there—listening to lyrics about sex, cheap romance and unhealthy relationships isn't going to get it done. Those songs are only going to muddle our thoughts and make us discontent.

- **Look back over the music you listed earlier. Do any of those types of music or specific songs keep you from preserving your whole heart for God and your future husband? List them here.**

- **I'm a big fan of music—it's not bad in and of itself. What types of music or specific songs could actually help you think about the right things?**

The reason I'm focusing on music is because we spend *so* much time listening to it. But the same principles apply to *anything* that causes your thoughts to run wild. Magazines, romance novels (or other books), certain websites—these all can be just as dangerous. A good rule of thumb: If you catch yourself about to do things that you should be doing *only* with your future husband, get away from whatever it is that encourages those thoughts.

- **Do any of the things that you watch or read for entertainment keep you from thinking about things that are true, lovely and worthy of praise? Which ones?**

- **Obviously, not all media is bad. What shows or movies have you seen that encourage you to save your whole heart for God and your future husband?**

Before we move on to the next chapter, I just want to mention that if you don't learn to control your thoughts now, they won't suddenly whip into shape when you're married. Learning to consciously decide what you will and won't think about is a lifelong discipline. The thoughts you struggle with may change—instead of trying not to daydream about guys, now I struggle not to daydream about my dream house, our future kids or a vacation in the Bahamas—but the principles are the same. If you can figure out how to keep your thoughts in check now, you'll save yourself a lot of heartache down the road.

Let's pray.

> *Gracious God, thank You for promising to forgive my sins when I bring them to You. I confess that my thoughts have been running wild and that those thoughts cause my emotions to get the better of me. Help me think on what is true, right, pure, lovely and worthy of praise. I want to be free of shame so that I can walk with dignity and make You proud. I love You, sweet Jesus, for making that possible. Amen.*

ten: doughnuts and snowballs

You may say, "I am allowed to do anything." But I reply, "Not everything is good for you."
And even though "I am allowed to do anything," I must not become a slave to anything.
1 Corinthians 6:12, *NLT*

It always happens.

Whenever I speak to girls on the topic of relationships, someone always asks (and everyone else in the room is wishing someone would ask) the classic question, "How far is too far?"

💬 **What do you think? Have you given any thought to that question? Have you come to any conclusions? What have your parents, youth pastor or big sis told you is "too far"?**

We'll answer that question a little later. But first, I have a confession to make.

SECRET LOVE

I *love* doughnuts. Not just any doughnuts, mind you—I'm talking about Krispy Kreme's choco-late-iced, Bavarian custard-filled doughnuts. The big shots at Krispy Kreme seriously outdid themselves on this one. I'm beginning to salivate just *thinking* about the moist, spongy outside and the creamy goodness inside, all topped with that delicious chocolate. *Mmm*—delicious!

Would it be wrong for me to drive down to the nearest Krispy Kreme right now and give in to my growing desire for this custard-filled treat? What if I ate one *every* day? Would that be wrong? Would it be a sin? (Don't worry, this isn't a trick question.) No! Enjoying a delicious treat isn't a sin (although allowing food to take God's place in our hearts is). But at a whop-ping 300 calories a piece, would eating a Krispy Kreme custard-filled doughnut every day be *good* for me? Not unless I consider heart disease my idea of a good time! Not even eating *one* doughnut would be good for me.

💬 **What tasty treats do you crave but avoid because you know they aren't good for you?**

Look back at 1 Corinthians 6:12. Paul totally nails it here. Even though I *could* eat as many doughnuts as I wanted, I know that isn't what's best for me or for my body. By refusing to give in to my cravings, I don't allow myself to become a slave to those delicious doughnuts.

At this point you may be wondering, *What in the world do doughnuts have to do with physical relationships?* Well, Paul was actually talking about sexual immorality in 1 Corinthians 6:12. He was explaining to the believers in Corinth that even though they would be forgiven for having gone too far physically, they would be crazy to let themselves become slaves to something so harmful. Here's the same verse, this time in the context of Paul's message.

> You may say, "I am allowed to do anything." But I reply, "Not everything is good for you." And even though "I am allowed to do anything," I must not become a slave to anything. . . . Our bodies were not made for sexual immorality. They were made for the Lord, and the Lord cares about our bodies. . . . Don't you realize that your bodies are actually parts of Christ? Run away from sexual sin! No other sin so clearly affects the body as this one does. For sexual immorality is a sin against your own body. Or don't you know that your body is the temple of the Holy Spirit, who lives in you and was given to you by God? You do not belong to yourself, for God bought you with a high price. So you must honor God with your body (1 Corinthians 6:12-15,18-20, NLT).

💬 **Summarize Paul's massage in your own words.**

💬 **Paul says that sexual sin is "a sin against your own body." How can going too far physically harm your body? How can it harm your emotions?**

- If going too far physically in a relationship is harmful to our bodies, minds and spirits, would a girl with dignity give in to sexual temptation? Why or why not?

SNOW DAYS

I live at the beach now, but growing up I was a born an' bred mountain girl. One of my favorite things about living in the mountains was "snow days." A snow day meant that all of us kids got a day off school because the roads were too snowy or too icy for the buses to come pick us up. Nothing beat the feeling of waking up to a thick blanket of snow, knowing that I could play in it all day and then come inside for some hot soup and games by the wood-burning stove. (Look at me, I'm getting all nostalgic!)

All those snow days made me somewhat of an expert on the fine art of playing in the snow. I discovered that wet snow is best for forts and snowballs because it sticks together better. With wet snow, you can take a snowball the size of a walnut, roll it down a long hill and watch it get bigger and bigger and bigger, until it's so big you can't lift it!

That's how a physical relationship works. Imagine for a minute that when you enter the world of dating, you start with a snowball the size of a walnut. When you hold hands with a guy for the first time, the snowball gets a little bigger. With each step—the first time you hug, the first time you kiss, the first time you cuddle—your snowball grows bigger and bigger, just as though it's being rolled down a long hill. You'd be surprised how easy it is for your snowball to grow out of control.

Unfortunately, if you break up with that boyfriend and get together with another one, you don't naturally start with a walnut-sized snowball with the second guy—you start wherever you left off in the first relationship. For example, if you were in the habit of kissing your first boyfriend, it will be that much easier to go there—and even further—with the next boyfriend.

- Think about the physical relationships you have had with guys (if any). How would you describe the size of your snowball right now? Could you hold it in your hand, or is it too heavy to lift?

💬 **The chances of teenaged romances lasting until marriage are pretty slim. So in light of the snowball illustration, why are physical relationships so dangerous?**

the better question

Okay, you've been patient long enough. It's time to reveal the better question. Instead of asking, *How far is too far?* ask yourself, *How far is* good *for me?* That's a question you have to answer on your own, but the following review of some of the lessons that we've learned so far about relationships will help you to come to the best possible answer.

- Sexual sin hurts you personally. It's a sin against your own body.
- Relationships are like cement. The more physical your relationship is, the faster the cement will dry (more on this in chapter 11).
- Your heart is like a water balloon. Each time you enter into a relationship, it's like poking a small hole in your heart. The more you do physically in a relationship, the bigger the hole you will make.
- Someday you will have to face your husband and own up to everything you've done with other guys.
- Just because something tastes good (such as custard-filled doughnuts) or feels good (such as physical intimacy) doesn't mean it's the best thing for you.
- Each step you take physically packs more snow onto your snowball, and it's easier than you think for that snowball to get out of control.
- A girl with dignity respects herself and her future husband enough to save her body and her heart for him.

The Bible is clear that having sex before marriage is wrong, but what about the in-between stuff? Not sure? Ask yourself whether hugging, kissing, cuddling—or whatever else you might want to do with a guy—is good for you, not whether it *feels* good (because it will). Ask yourself whether it will glorify God and help you keep your heart pure for your future husband. If you're ever unsure about where to draw the line, ask yourself whether you would do that in front of your future husband. Remember, you belong to him, even before you marry him!

● It's best to decide how far you will go physically *before* you get into a relationship—definitely before you're alone in a dark place!—while your mind is thinking more clearly. Spend several minutes in prayer asking God to help you formulate physical boundaries that will keep your heart pure for your future husband, and then write down what you decide.

location, location
location

Now that you've set some physical boundaries, let's talk about the best ways to make sure that you're empowered to stick to your guns, because a girl who respects herself doesn't compromise what's best for her. First, let's talk about location.

Strangely enough, I was never tempted to cross the physical boundaries I had set when I was hanging out with a guy in the living room with my parents, at youth group, or in other public places. The problems arose when we chose to play with fire by hanging out *alone* and *in the dark*—a bad combination. The locations and settings you choose will either make or break your attempts at purity.

Let's play a game called "Smart or Stupid." It goes like this: I'll describe three different scenarios, and you tell me whether each option would be smart or stupid for a girl who's trying to stick to her guns.

Scenario 1—Rick and Julie have been going out for a few months, and their parents have agreed to let them go out on their first date alone. After the movie, Rick asks Julie if she wants to go park by the lake so they can "talk" before he drives her home.

Smart   Stupid

Scenario 2—Tanya's parents are at an out-of-town conference and won't be home until really late. She's pretty bored, so she considers calling her boyfriend, Nate, to see whether he wants to come keep her company.

Smart   Stupid

Scenario 3—Tyler and Marianna are in Tyler's room working on homework. Marianna doesn't think it's a big deal because Tyler's parents are downstairs watching TV. But after a while, Tyler doesn't seem interested in doing homework. Marianna considers saying, "Hey, why don't we head downstairs and watch TV with your parents."

Smart   Stupid

💬 **What places or situations tend to get you into physical trouble? How can you avoid these places or situations in the future?**

💬 **Talk to God for a few minutes and ask Him to help you think of creative ways that you can spend time with your boyfriend without being tempted to compromise the physical boundaries that you wrote down earlier. Write your ideas below.**

A CLOSING THOUGHT

Our society (and especially the media) cheapen physical intimacy and make it hard for us to focus on saving our whole hearts for marriage instead of pushing the envelope every chance we get. I hope that this chapter has helped you come to some conclusions about what a girl with dignity will and won't do physically.

God wants us to enjoy our teen years! He's not some cosmic killjoy who's intent on ruining all our fun. Ecclesiastes 11:9 says, "Be happy, young [woman], while you are young, and let your heart give you joy in the days of your youth. Follow the ways of your heart and whatever your eyes see, but know that for all these things God will bring you to judgment." In other words, enjoy being young—but remember that you will have to own up to everything you do and that God sees *everything*.

Unfortunately, I focused too much on following the ways of my heart and not enough on the consequences of the foolish things I did. This is a poem I wrote for my future husband when I finally realized that I had been a fool to give so much of myself away. It's not the best poem I've ever written, but it expresses the sorrow and regret I felt after going too far physically in several relationships. I share it in the hopes that it will help keep you from needlessly traveling that same road.

To My Beloved

My heart is grieved,
My soul consumed with dismay,
For the lost pieces of my heart
So carelessly given away.
Precious pieces of me,
Meant for you alone;
My love for you, I confess,
I have not always shown.
I never stopped to think
That my heart wasn't mine;
I was only concerned
With not tripping over "the line."

Now I see my folly—
The line was never there!
ALL of me was meant for you,
Not a piece was meant to share!
Today I realize my mistake,
And I ask you to forgive:
Selflessly, faithfully, purely,
From this moment on,
I promise to live.

Beautiful Savior, thank You for paying the high price to purchase me as Your own. I know that my body is now part of Your body and that I am one with You in spirit. I want the choices I make and the relationships I have to be a reflection of our relationship. Give me the strength and resolve to refuse to do anything that isn't what's best for me. I love You. Amen.

ten tips for a
happy, healthy heart

A happy heart makes the face cheerful, but heartache crushes the spirit.
Proverbs 15:13

I love the simple truth found in this verse. When our hearts are happy, our faces show it—usually with a big teeth-filled grin. But when our hearts are broken, the deepest part of our being feels crushed, as though a mammoth dinosaur decided to use our heart as a breakfast stool.

It should be a no-brainer, then, that avoiding unnecessary heartbreak is a good thing. Who wants to be flattened under a dinosaur's buttocks? I'll take the big smiley face, thank you very much!

Have you ever had your heart broken in a relationship? What happened? How did it feel? What did you learn from the experience?

As I hesitatingly mentioned a couple chapters back, I've had my heart broken more than my fair share. But by the grace of God, I did learn quite a bit through those rough experiences, and I'd like to share some of those bits of wisdom with you so that you can avoid the pain and heartache that comes with doing relationships the *wrong* way. Whether you're interested in dating guys now or have decided to wait until you're older (either by choice or by parental decree), I hope these tips will help you maintain a happy, healthy heart.

tip 1:
glorify God

To give glory to God basically means to make Him look good. Remember from chapter 7 that being a follower of Christ is like being an Olympian—we're called to a higher standard so that we don't bring shame to our Coach or to our countrymen. So what makes God look good? Philippians 1:11 (*NLT*) reads, "May you always be filled with the fruit of your salvation—those good things that are produced in your life by Jesus Christ—for this will bring much glory and praise to God." In other words, if you see anything in your relationship—emotionally, spiritually or physically—that wasn't "produced in your life by Jesus Christ," you've got some more training to do!

> **What specific ways could you make God look good in a romantic relationship? How could a relationship disgrace God and your fellow believers?**

tip 2:
don't date unbelievers

This tip is pretty simple. If the guy you like isn't a Christian, don't get into a relationship with him. If you're already dating a non-Christian, get out of it quick. The longer you wait, the harder it will be. A relationship is a lot like cement—the more time you allow that cement to dry, the harder and more emotionally destructive it will be to break things off.

This may seem too cut and dry, but the Bible doesn't mince words on this topic, so neither will I. Second Corinthians 6:14 (*THE MESSAGE*) says, "Don't become partners with those who reject God. How can you make a partnership out of right and wrong? That's not partnership; that's war. Is light best friends with dark?" If you're not willing to follow this simple command from the God who rescued you from death—you know, the One you owe *everything* to—then maybe you don't love Him as much as you say you do. Besides, I've seen from personal experience and by watching friends and loved ones that God knows what He's talking about. (Imagine that!)

💬 Why do you think God makes such a big point of us not dating (let alone marrying) someone who does not share our passion for godliness? Do you trust God enough to steer clear of unbelievers, even if you think the guy is *really* cool and nice and respectful?

tip 3:
practice biblical love

Pull out your Bible and read 1 Corinthians 13:4-8. Although this definition of love should be in every part of our lives and not just in romantic relationships, our dating relationships are great practice grounds to work on being selfless, forgiving, truthful and Christ-focused. Then, if and when you marry, you'll be a real pro at selfless, biblical, God-honoring love.

💬 Look back over 1 Corinthians 13:4-8. Which parts of true, biblical love are hardest for you to practice? What can you do to get better at loving others the way that God loves you?

tip 4:
keep an open mind

The honest truth is that no matter how serious you are about a guy in junior high or high school, there's an overwhelming chance that you'll break up before you're old enough to marry. I'm not trying to be pessimistic here—I'm just looking at the statistics. Of course, when you're wild-eyed and ga-ga over a guy, the last thing that you want to hear is that he might not be the one. But if you want to keep a happy, healthy heart and avoid the pain of having that heart broken, *be realistic from the start.* Make time for others—don't make him your life. Don't throw all your emotions into the relationship; always remember that if you do break up, it's not the end of the world. Trust me! As much as I hate the cliché, there are in fact *tons* of fish in the big ocean of life, and you have a lot of life to live!

💬 **Look up James 4:13-15. How does this verse apply to keeping an open mind while dating?**

💬 **Practically speaking, how can a girl keep from getting so emotionally involved in a relationship that her world explodes when she and her boyfriend break up?**

tip 5:
keep your eyes open

Tip 5 is similar to tip 4. Smart, self-respecting girls don't allow themselves to become blind with love, no matter how perfect they think a guy is. If you keep your mind clear and your eyes open, you'll be much more likely to recognize any red flags in the relationship, such as the following:

- Excessive anger
- Sexual pressure
- Disrespect to you and/or others
- No spiritual growth
- Crude language or sexual jokes
- Extreme jealousy or controlling tendencies
- Violence

Ultimately, the whole point of dating is to find a husband who will love you with God's kind of love and treat you right. So if your boyfriend acts, speaks or treats you in ways that you would consider out of the question in a husband, don't ignore the problems because you're "just" dating.

On the flip side, part of keeping your eyes open in a relationship means looking for the *good* qualities too! Make mental notes of the things you really like about your boyfriend so that in the event your relationship doesn't work out, you'll have a much better idea of what to look for in the future. Here are some great qualities to watch for:

- Passion for God
- Respect for you and for others
- Integrity
- Honesty
- Desire to grow in Christ
- Purity

💬 If you're in a relationship now, have you noticed any red flags? What are they? What good qualities that you'd like to see in your future husband does your boyfriend possess? If you're not in a relationship right now, what qualities are non-negotiable in a potential boyfriend?

tip 6: always keep your future husband in mind

Now that I'm married, I can't stress this tip enough. As impossible as it seems, one day you will marry the man you've been waiting and praying for. In the meantime, don't do *anything*—physically or emotionally—that you'll regret telling him later. Song of Solomon 6:3 (*NKJV*) says, "I am my beloved's, and my beloved is mine." Never forget that you are already spoken for, girl!

One of the best ways to keep your heart focused on that hope is to write love letters (yes, love letters!)—but not to your boyfriend or to your latest crush. These notes of love are for your *future husband* only. Tell him how much you long for him, what you pray for him and why you are saving your heart, mind and body for him. (It doesn't matter whether you have a boyfriend or not—it's not like you'd be cheating on him!) Imagine the joy it would bring you and your groom to present him with all those letters on your wedding day! I can't imagine a better wedding gift. And what better way to keep your heart focused on him in the meantime!

tip 7:
pray for wisdom

We have a habit of excluding God from decisions about love. We have no problem asking Him for help on a history test or for that new cell phone, but when it comes to issues that *really* matter, we leave Him completely out of the equation.

If you want to avoid getting your heart broken, ask God for wisdom. Ask Him whether a relationship you are considering would be the best thing for you or whether you're interested in the guy for the wrong reasons. God promises to give us all the wisdom we need, as long as we don't doubt that He'll give us an answer (see James 1:5-8). I would add that you also have to be willing to hear whatever answer He gives—not just what you *want* to hear. It's so easy to pray, *Lord, show me what to do,* and then only look for signs that support what you've already decided.

> Do you involve God in your decisions about guys, relationships and love? If not, why? What can you do to start seeking His wisdom?

tip 8:
listen to advice

When we ask God for wisdom in a relationship, He has a funny way of speaking through people around us, such as parents, godly friends or a big sis. Here again, we have to resist the temptation to only hear what people say when it supports what we want to do. Part of keeping an open mind (tip 4) is listening to advice—no matter how painful—from those who care about us. Proverbs 27:6 says, "Wounds from a friend can be trusted, but an enemy multiplies kisses." I'll take painfully honest advice over meaningless flattery any day.

For some reason, we have the hardest time listening to our parents' advice. I guess we think they're too old to know what we're feeling. Right now, I'm in a strange, in-between stage in life. I'm not old enough to have teenaged children of my own, but I am old enough to see that back then my parents knew me *way* better than I knew myself in a lot of ways. Not only that,

I'm also beginning to see that God put my parents in authority over me to *protect* my heart, not to keep me from getting married until I was 40 (though my dad did threaten that on more than one occasion!). What I'm trying to say is that even if it doesn't seem like it now, your parents truly have your best interests in mind, so trust their judgment. God promises good things to those who respect their parents' wishes (see Exodus 20:12).

- Proverbs 13:20 reads, "He who walks with the wise grows wise, but a companion of fools suffers harm." Are your friends wise? Do they give you wise advice, or do they tell you what they think you want to hear?

- What kind of a friend are you?

tip 9:
observe other guy friends

Whether or not you're in a relationship, it's a good idea to observe the guys around you. Take mental notes of the good qualities that you would like in a husband. Learn all you can by watching guys with their friends, girlfriends or wives. Proverbs 13:16 says that a wise man (or in this case, woman) acts out of knowledge. You'll make the best decision in a future mate if you've been gathering the facts all along.

- Think about the guy friends and godly men that you know. What sort of qualities do you see in them that you think you would like in a husband? (For example, they have a sense of humor, good manners, or are honest.)

tip 10:
discover your true identity

My last word of advice on how to have a healthy, happy heart is to discover your true identity. Become the type of girl who will attract the *right* kind of guy—the kind of guy who embodies all of the qualities you deserve. Bottom line: Become more and more like Christ. You can't go wrong with that! Discovering your identity also means figuring out your likes, dislikes, passions, goals, dreams and standards. Once you are head over heels for a guy, it's really easy to become whatever he's looking for, so be secure in who you are first.

Proverbs 31:10-31 describes what marks the kind of godly wife that a quality guy wants. At first read, she may sound a bit old-fashioned, but look closely—she's kind, hard-working, inventive, loving, dignified, self-respecting and godly. Developing these qualities is a sure-fire way to attract a grade-A, awesome, God-honoring guy.

💬 **As we close this chapter, use this space to write a prayer to God. Share with Him your fears and your dreams about love and romance. Ask Him to keep molding you into the godly young woman who will someday attract the right kind of husband.**

Wait for the Lord; be strong and take heart and wait for the Lord.
Psalm 27:14

The righteous cry out, and the Lord hears them; he delivers them from all their troubles.
The Lord is close to the brokenhearted and saves those who are crushed in spirit.
Psalm 34:17-18

We've talked a lot about love, respect, dignity and purity over the past few chapters, and I pray that God has planted a dream in your heart that will stand the test of time. Before we close, I want to share with you how God planted a dream of true love in my broken heart, bringing hope out of the mess I had made of my love life. I don't know where you've been or where you are now, but I do know that if God can make a crumbled heart like mine whole again, He can restore your heart too.

- **Have you done a good job of saving your whole heart for God and your future husband, or do you feel like you've made a mess of your heart by giving away too many pieces of yourself? Explain how you feel and what has caused you to feel that way.**

- **Do you wonder whether the things you've done are beyond God's forgiveness or whether your heart has been hurt too deeply for even God to heal? Talk to God about those feelings. Don't worry—you can't shock Him! Just be honest.**

THE RING

I wrote this journal entry on April 2, 2000, from a hillside overlooking the Sea of Galilee in Israel (I studied a few months there in college). The sun was shining, the green grass was studded with thousands of dazzlingly white daisies, and all was right with the world—except, of course, for my muddled, confused heart. Having carelessly given my heart away once again (you'd think a girl would learn!), I knew that something needed to change. A couple weeks before I found myself in Galilee, I had purchased a ring in Jerusalem. I had the Hebrew letters of Song of Solomon 6:3 (*NASB*) carved into the silver band: "I am my beloved's and my beloved is mine." This is what I wrote.

אני לדודי ודודי לי

adorns my ring finger. The silver Hebrew letters catch the sun and my attention. I contemplate the meaning of those words as I hike down the Arbell Cliffs overlooking the Sea of Galilee. "I am my beloved's." . . . What exactly does that mean? A replay of sinful seaweed surfaces in the churning waters of the "sea of forgetfulness" and a tinge of shame causes me to close my eyes. "I am my beloved's." I am not mine. With a warm breeze blowing across the green meadow below, I realize what it is I need to do—or rather, not do. And instead of suppressing the Holy Spirit's prodding once again, I accept the challenge He presents me. From this moment on, I wait in anticipation of the first time my lips will be kissed by "my beloved." I will save every piece of my heart for him alone—because I love him enough to sacrifice temporary pleasure for him. Although at times I know I'll struggle, I believe the Lord will give me the strength and discipline to save every remaining piece of me for the one I'll love more passionately, more selflessly, more deeply than any before him. Until then, my lips shall remain rational, pure, and MINE! Lord God, give me the strength. I know it is only through the power of Your Holy Spirit that I can overcome the temptations ahead. I love You, Lord, and I make this vow for Your glory alone.

I wish I could say that when I made that promise to God, angels descended from heaven, trumpets blew and a magic carpet whisked me away to unite me with "my beloved" and we instantly lived happily ever after. That would have been nice, but God had other plans. In fact, the road that lay ahead of me was *really* difficult. I wasn't perfect along the way, but—in nothing short of a miracle—God did help me honor that vow. After years of mistakes, shame, broken hearts and shattered dreams, I lived the years after that day in Galilee waiting for my husband. And when God finally brought us together and we first kissed—well, let's just say it was *totally* worth the wait!

I'm not suggesting that you make a vow to God promising not to kiss anyone but your husband—unless that's something He's calling *you* to do. I simply share my story with you in the hopes that if you, like me, feel as if the water in your balloon drained out long ago, you can know that it's *never* to late for purity; it's never too late to walk with dignity and respect. I'm a living example of the power of crying out to God for forgiveness and waiting on Him to restore the dreams of romance and true love in a heart.

Isaiah 43:18-19 brought me so much peace and reassurance during that time of transformation. They are words of comfort that God spoke to the nation of Israel.

> Forget the former things; do not dwell on the past. See, I am doing a new thing!
> Now it springs up; do you not perceive it? I am making a way in the desert and
> streams in the wasteland.

- **What evidence do you see in your life that God is doing a "new thing" in your heart?**

- **Are you tempted to dwell in the past? Why do you think that is? How can you leave the past behind you?**

- **What might God be calling you to do or to give up so that He can preserve or restore the dream in your heart? (It might not be anything dramatic. Just be open to whatever He might ask of you.)**

ONE FINE DAY

I'm so glad that God has let me be a part of the beautiful work He's doing in your heart. No matter how long or difficult the road seems, wait for God's timing. He wants to give you the best gift imaginable! Don't cheapen that gift by trying to peak under the wrapping paper. He knows exactly what journey you need to take to become the beautiful woman of dignity He wants you to be.

This is a poem I wrote in anticipation of someday getting to the end of my quest for love. Although I wrote it long before I knew whom I would marry, it was almost like a prophecy of things to come. Every word came true!

February Prayer

So long I've waited,
So many tears I've cried,
Waiting for that someone
To be forever by my side.
Someone who sees me
For who I am inside,
Someone all my hopes and fears
With whom I can confide.
I knew You had a plan, God,
Though I was blind to see—
Now before me is the answer
To that beautiful mystery.
You promised if I'd trust,
You'd show me the way;
It brings tears to my eyes
To see him standing here today.
How could I have doubted
Your perfect, sovereign will?
All You ever wanted was
My deepest needs to fill.
Now You have blessed me
With a little taste of You,
And my earnest prayer shall be
That to You we will be true.

The next two pages of journal space are for you. You can write a prayer, a song, a letter—whatever will express the hopes and dreams that God has restored to your heart and your resolve to save your heart for the man who will fulfill all those dreams. Look back on these pages often, especially when you're tempted to call it quits. Trust me—he will be worth the wait!

Let's pray.

> God, You are full of grace and mercy. Thank You for doing a new thing in my life. Even now I can begin to feel Your cool stream watering the desert of my heart. I know that everything is possible with You—including a new, whole, restored heart. I give You all my mistakes, hopes, dreams and fears, and I trust that You know what's best for me. May Your will be done in my life. Amen.

More Breakthrough Books from Soul Sister and Soul Survivor